Introducing Spring Framework 6

Learning and Building Java-based Applications With Spring

Second Edition

Felipe Gutierrez
Joseph B. Ottinger

Apress®

Introducing Spring Framework 6: Learning and Building Java-based Applications With Spring

Felipe Gutierrez
Cary, NC, USA

Joseph B. Ottinger
YOUNGSVILLE, NC, USA

ISBN-13 (pbk): 978-1-4842-8636-4
https://doi.org/10.1007/978-1-4842-8637-1

ISBN-13 (electronic): 978-1-4842-8637-1

Managing Director, Apress Media LLC: Welmoed Spahr
Acquisitions Editor: Steve Anglin
Development Editor: Laura Berendson
Coordinating Editor: Jill Balzano

Cover designed by eStudioCalamar

Cover image by Mink Mingle on Unsplash (www.unsplash.com)

Distributed to the book trade worldwide by Apress Media, LLC, 1 New York Plaza, New York, NY 10004, U.S.A. Phone 1-800-SPRINGER, fax (201) 348-4505, e-mail orders-ny@springer-sbm.com, or visit www.springeronline.com. Apress Media, LLC is a California LLC and the sole member (owner) is Springer Science + Business Media Finance Inc (SSBM Finance Inc). SSBM Finance Inc is a **Delaware** corporation.

For information on translations, please e-mail booktranslations@springernature.com; for reprint, paperback, or audio rights, please e-mail bookpermissions@springernature.com.

Apress titles may be purchased in bulk for academic, corporate, or promotional use. eBook versions and licenses are also available for most titles. For more information, reference our Print and eBook Bulk Sales web page at http://www.apress.com/bulk-sales.

Any source code or other supplementary material referenced by the author in this book is available to readers on GitHub (https://github.com/Apress). For more detailed information, please visit http://www.apress.com/source-code.

Printed on acid-free paper

To my parents, Rocio Cruz and Felipe Gutierrez.

—Felipe Gutierrez

To my beloved wife and sons, and to the rabbits that keep hounding my yard.

—Joseph B. Ottinger

Table of Contents

About the Authors..ix

About the Technical Reviewer xi

Acknowledgments xiii

Introduction xv

Part I: Spring Framework Basics...1

Chapter 1: Your First Spring Application 3

    Pre-requirements... 4

    Source Code Organization.. 5

    Hello World Example 10

    Hello, Boot... 14

    Hello, Kotlin 18

    Summary.. 21

Chapter 2: Working with Classes and Dependencies 23

    The "My Documents" Application 23

    Testing the Implementation 28

    Testing with Spring 32

    Summary.. 35

Chapter 3: Applying Different Configurations 37

    Testing My Documents... 37

    Annotation Configuration in Spring 45

        Component Scanning 47

    XML Configuration in Spring 50

        Expanding the Configuration 53

Component Scanning in XML 58

Is XML Configuration a Good Idea? 59

Choosing a Configuration Approach 60

Summary 61

Chapter 4: Using Bean Scopes 63

Scope 63

The Scopes 63

Using the Scopes 65

Annotations 73

Summary 74

Chapter 5: Using Resource Files 75

Injecting a Resource 75

Loading Injected Values from Property Files 78

Internationalization 81

Summary 85

Part II: The Spring Framework 87

Chapter 6: Adding Simple Persistence to Your Spring Application 89

Persistence As a Concept 89

Revisiting Our Simple Data Model 90

Choosing a Database 93

Setting Up a JDBC Connection 94

The JDBCTemplate 99

Our Service Interfaces and the SearchEngine Implementation 100

Tying It All Together 104

Summary 106

Chapter 7: Letting Spring Build Your Data Access Objects 107

The Project 107

Spring Data Repositories 113

Summary 118

Chapter 8: Showing Your Spring Application on the Web **119**

Thymeleaf 124

Tying It All Together 128

Summary 132

Part III: Advanced Techniques with Spring Framework **133**

Chapter 9: Integrating Your Spring Application with External Systems **135**

The Process 136

Summary 146

Chapter 10: Exposing a REST API **147**

What Is REST? 147

Building a REST API in Spring 148

Summary 164

Chapter 11: Sending Emails from Within Spring **165**

Sending Email 165

    Set Up MailTrap 166

    The Email Aspect of the Project 168

Asynchronous Tasks in Spring 180

Adding Scheduling Events in Spring 182

Summary 190

Part IV: The New Spring I/O **191**

Chapter 12: Using Dynamic Languages **193**

Loading Functionality Dynamically with Groovy 194

    The Simplest Dynamic MessageService 196

    Using Spring to Configure the Dynamic MessageService 200

    Inline Dynamic Content 202

Summary 204

TABLE OF CONTENTS

Chapter 13: Where Do You Go From Here?.. **205**

Spring and the Impact on Development.. 205

The Wider World of Spring 207

Index.. **209**

About the Authors

Felipe Gutierrez is a solutions software architect, with a bachelor's and a master's degree in computer science from Instituto Tecnologico y de Estudios Superiores de Monterrey Campus Ciudad de Mexico, with over 20 years of IT experience, during which time he developed programs for companies in multiple vertical industries, such as government, retail, healthcare, education, and banking. He is currently working as a principal technical instructor for Pivotal, specializing in Cloud Foundry, Spring Framework, Spring Cloud Native Applications, Groovy, and RabbitMQ, among other technologies. He has worked as a solutions architect for big companies like Nokia, Apple, Redbox, and Qualcomm, among others. He is also the author of *Introducing Spring Framework*, *Pro Spring Boot*, and *Spring Boot Messaging*, all published by Apress.

Joseph B. Ottinger is reputedly an expert software developer, coder, and programmer with experience covering many technologies and platforms. He was the Editor in Chief for both *Java Developer Journal* and TheServerSide.com and has contributed to a large number of publications, open source projects, and commercial products over the years, using many different languages (but primarily Java, Python, and JavaScript). He is the author of *Hibernate Recipes* and *Beginning Hibernate* for Apress and has authored other books as well as a few articles here and there. He's also constantly writing odes to random furry creatures grooving in caves with members of ancient cultures, or something.

About the Technical Reviewer

 **Manuel Jordan Elera** is an autodidactic developer and researcher who enjoys learning new technologies for his own experiments and creating new integrations. Manuel won the Springy Award 2013 Community Champion and Spring Champion. In his little free time, he reads the Bible and composes music on his guitar. Manuel is known as dr_pompeii. He has tech-reviewed numerous books, including *Pro Spring MVC with WebFlux* (Apress, 2020), *Pro Spring Boot 2* (Apress, 2019), *Rapid Java Persistence and Microservices* (Apress, 2019), *Java Language Features* (Apress, 2018), *Spring Boot 2 Recipes* (Apress, 2018), and *Java APIs, Extensions and Libraries* (Apress, 2018). You can read his detailed tutorials on Spring technologies and contact him through his blog at www.manueljordanelera.blogspot.com. You can follow Manuel on his Twitter account, @dr_pompeii.

Acknowledgments

I would like to express all my gratitude to the Apress team: first and foremost to Steve Anglin for accepting my proposal; Laura Berendson and Jill Balzaono for helping me out when I needed it; and the rest of the Apress team involved in this project. Thanks to everybody for making this possible.

Thanks to our technical reviewer, Manuel Jordan, and the entire Spring team for making the Spring Framework the best programming and configuration model for modern Java-based enterprise applications.

Thanks to my parents, Rocio Cruz and Felipe Gutierrez, for all their love and support, and to my best friend, my brother Edgar Gerardo Gutierrez. Even though we live far away, we are closer than ever; thanks, "macnitous."

—Felipe Gutierrez

I'm constantly amazed that I'm asked to write these acknowledgments and dedications, mostly because they feel so limiting to point out only specific persons and events to whom I'm grateful. I would like to thank both grammar and spelling, and my sense of restraint in using both proper grammar *and* spelling in doing so, as well as the patience of my wife and family (and friends), without whom I'd hardly ever be able to do anything. This book was written to the tune of many classic '70s tunes, many of which were cheesy soft rock for some reason, and I'd like to thank a whole host of one-hit-wonders without which I'd never wonder what the record industry was thinking back then. It's awesome, and I miss it. May all of us live with as much love in our hearts for each other as we can stand.

—Joseph B. Ottinger

Introduction

This book is an introduction to the well-known Spring Framework that offers an inversion of control container for the Java platform. The Spring Framework is an open source application framework that can be used with any Java application.

After reading this book, you will know how to do the following:

- Use the Spring Framework efficiently.

- Add persistence through JDBC databases, with an easy migration to NoSQL.

- Do unit and integration testing.

- Create web applications and expose RESTful APIs.

- Send messages via JMS, a model that extends to AMQP, RabbitMQ, and MQTT.

- Use dynamic languages like Groovy, Ruby, and Bean Shell for Spring.

- Use Groovy with Spring.

- Use the new Spring Boot and Spring XD technologies.

Who This Book Is For

Introducing Spring Framework 6 is a hands-on guide for any developer who is new to the Spring Framework and wants to learn how to build applications with it. Within this book you will find all the necessary elements to create enterprise-ready applications by using the Spring Framework and all its features and modules.

How This Book Is Organized

This book uses a simple **My Documents** application that you will develop incrementally over the course of the book. The book consists of the following four parts:

- Part 1: Spring Framework Basics: You will learn about the dependency injection design pattern, and Spring's container implementation and how it will help you create a better design by programming toward interfaces. You'll learn the different configurations that you can apply to the Spring Framework. You will also learn how to use bean scopes, work with collections and resource files, and how to test your Spring applications.

- Part 2: The Spring Framework: You will learn to add persistence and integrate your Spring application with other systems. And you will be able to add your Spring application to the Web.

- Part 3: Advanced Techniques with Spring Framework: You will learn how to use message brokers with Spring for massive scalability and distributed architecture, how to expose your application using a RESTful API, and how to send emails and schedule events in your application.

- Part 4: The New Spring I/O: You will learn how to integrate Spring and Groovy into your Spring application. You'll also get pointers on where to look for further technologies in your journey with Spring.

Source Code

All source code used in this book can be found at github.com/apress/introducing-spring-framework6. Included in this download will be the following online-only appendixes:

- Installing Java and Gradle for your Operating System

- Other Recommended Tools

With all that said, let's go ahead and start with the Spring Framework!

PART I

Spring Framework Basics

CHAPTER 1

Your First Spring Application

Most books start with a very long explanation about the technology they are using, the history of it, and often a small example that you can't run until you reach later chapters. In this book, I am going to take a different approach. I am going to start with some basic examples, and I will explain in detail what they do and how to use them so that you get to know Spring quickly. The examples in this chapter will show you how easy it is to integrate the Spring Framework into any existing project or how to start one from scratch and modify it without any effort.

Figure 1-1 shows the Spring portfolio website (`https://spring.io`). In this website, you can find all of the Spring Extensions, guides, and documentation to help you understand better the Spring ecosystem. The Spring Framework itself can be found at `https://spring.io/projects/spring-framework`, if you're interested in drilling down already.

3

© Felipe Gutierrez, Joseph B. Ottinger 2022
F. Gutierrez and J. B. Ottinger, *Introducing Spring Framework 6*, https://doi.org/10.1007/978-1-4842-8637-1_1

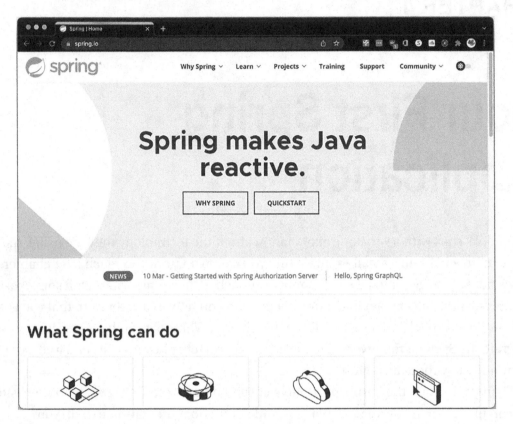

Figure 1-1. `https://spring.io`

Pre-requirements

In order to start with the first Spring Framework example, we need to have some tools installed.

- You need the Java Development Kit (JDK) installed and configured, accessible on the command line. Unlike previous versions of Spring, which supported a wide range of Java versions, Spring 6 requires Java 17 or higher. There are many sites that provide Java 17, but the most appropriate will be either Adoptium's distribution page, at `https://adoptium.net/releases.html`, or Oracle's site, at `www.oracle.com/java/technologies/downloads/`, either of which are appropriate. You can also install Java via SDKMan! if you're on OSX (see `https://sdkman.io`).

- We're going to use the Gradle Build Tool, found at `https://gradle.org`, for the book (See Figure 1-2). Gradle is one of the two most popular and capable build tools for the JVM; choosing Gradle here is done mostly because it has very simple and short build scripts. We use a build tool because it's very much standard practice and gives us easy dependency management and a full build lifecycle, including the ability to run tests as part of our build; Gradle is also the tool of choice of the Spring team itself.

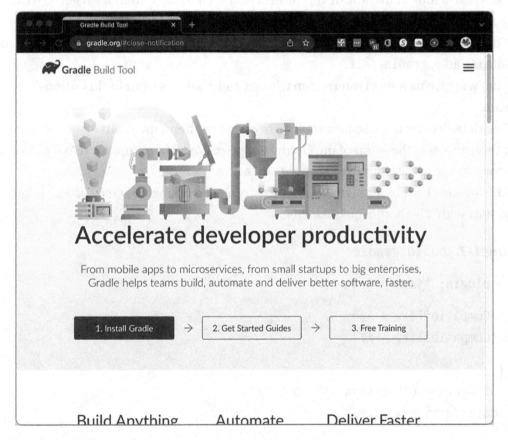

Figure 1-2. *The Gradle Website*

Source Code Organization

We're going to be looking at a lot of source code in this book.

This part will describe how it's laid out so it's easy to understand what is going where.

The book is going to be organized as a Gradle project, with various subdirectories.[1] Most of the subdirectories will be "modules" of the project, although there will be exceptions.

The top-level project needs its own directory; for the authors, it's the isf6 directory (for "Introducing Spring 6"). Most of the chapters' code will be in a clearly named directory mapping to the chapter number: thus, chapter02, chapter03, and so forth.

If a chapter has two separate projects, they'll be named with the chapter and then a description of the project, like `chapter01-hello-world` and `chapter01-hello-boot`.

Let's take a look at the "top-level" project and set it up, and then we'll get to writing some actual code that uses Spring.

The first thing we need to do, after installing Java and Gradle, is run a command to initialize Gradle, `gradle init`.

That will give us a short interaction where Gradle asks us what build options we want.

The defaults are fine, because we'll be overwriting them; the main result we want from this process is the setup of the Gradle wrapper. We want to replace two files in this directory, `build.gradle` and `settings.gradle`.

The top-level `build.gradle` file – in your "project working directory," so all relative paths start with "." – should look like this:

Listing 1-1. `build.gradle`

```
apply plugin: 'java'

sourceCompatibility = 17
targetCompatibility = 17

ext {
    springFrameworkVersion = "6.0.0-M4"
    testNgVersion = "7.6.1"
}
```

---

[1] Gradle uses a wrapper that downloads a copy of Gradle for each project. This is very useful for repeatable builds, but it creates a copy of Gradle on your hard drive for each project. As a result, it's far more efficient for us to have a single project for the book, rather than a project for each chapter, although some chapters will have separate projects, such as the `chapter-01-hello-boot` project.

```
allprojects {
    apply plugin: 'java'

    repositories {
        maven {
            url "https://repo.spring.io/milestone"
        }
        maven {
            url "https://repo.spring.io/snapshot"
            mavenContent {
                snapshotsOnly()
            }
        }
        mavenCentral()
    }

    dependencies {
        implementation \
        "ch.qos.logback:logback-classic:1.2.11"
        testImplementation \
        "org.testng:testng:$testNgVersion"
    }

    test {
        useTestNG()
    }
}
```

This file looks like a lot – but it's also one of the longer build files we'll have.

What it's doing is telling Gradle that we have a Java project (therefore, use the Java compiler), what level of Java to require (17, the current long-term support release as of writing and a requirement for Spring 6), a set of properties to provide version information to the build, and then a set of things that all projects should do: they're all Java projects, they all should pull dependencies from a set of external locations, and they should all rely on the TestNG testing framework.

The next file we'll want to overwrite is the settings.gradle file.

What this one does is describe the subprojects to include in the "main build." This one will change as we develop the content in the book.

Our `settings.gradle` needs to do two things:

1. Configure our project so it can find the plug-ins we'll want.

2. Configure the submodules for our book's content.

As this book is being written, Spring 6 has *not* been released. As a result, we need to use repositories that aren't "official releases." We already see the references to milestone and snapshot repositories in our `build.gradle`, but Gradle resolves dependencies and plug-ins through different mechanisms; thus, we need to configure them separately.

After the preamble for plug-in resolution – the bit that starts with `pluginManagement` – we have a simple way to name the project as a whole (`isf6`), and then we include our first subproject, the `chapter01-hello-spring` module. We'll be adding to this as we proceed through the book.[2]

We're going to start off with a simple "Hello, world" project, with a project name of `chapter01-hello-world`, so our `settings.gradle` file will be simple to start off with.

Listing 1-2. `settings.gradle`

```
pluginManagement {
    repositories {
        maven {
            url "https://repo.spring.io/milestone"
        }
        maven {
            url "https://repo.spring.io/snapshot"
            mavenContent {
                snapshotsOnly()
            }
        }
        gradlePluginPortal()
    }
}
```

------

[2] If you're looking at the source download, you'll see that the `settings.gradle` has a lot more to it and starts with a `//tag::chapter01[]` comment. These comments are to help format the book, which used the *actual source code* for listings instead of copied source.

```
rootProject.name = 'isf6'
include 'chapter01-hello-world'
```

There are two ways chapters will be represented in the source tree.

If the chapter's code is able to be represented cleanly with a single build, the chapter will be named in its own subdirectory, like chapter02, chapter03, and so forth.

However, if the chapter actually has two build processes, each build will get its own directory, with the chapter name being part of the name.

Oddly enough, this chapter will have two builds, so it will end up with chapter01-hello-world and chapter01-hello-boot, as an example.

The source organization for each chapter will follow the Gradle source code standard.

All source files go in a subdirectory called src, with (usually) two directories under that: main and test.

In each of those, there will be a directory corresponding to a source language (like java) or named resources, to map to source files that don't need compilation.

Under those directories, you'll see source files organized by Java packaging conventions.

Thus, after we create the structure for chapter01-hello-world, we have this directory tree as shown in Figure 1-3, assuming we have some Java source files in place already:

```
.
├── build.gradle
├── chapter01-hello-world
│   ├── build.gradle
│   └── src
│       └── main
│           └── java
│               └── chapter01
│                   ├── Application.java
│                   ├── HelloWorldMessageService.java
│                   └── MessageService.java
├── gradlew
├── gradlew.bat
└── settings.gradle
```

Figure 1-3. *The Directory Tree So Far*

Hello World Example

We've mentioned the chapter01-hello-world project enough. Let's take a look at what it actually has in it.

It's a great way to make sure your tools are set up properly, with an application that has no intrinsic value of its own (although it's worth having something say "Hello" to you, presumably).

Let's get the plumbing out of the way first and take a look at the build.gradle for chapter01-hello-world.

It's very simple: all it does is specify that our source code depends on spring-core and spring-context[3] and it uses a placeholder to pull in the specific version of the dependency, from the ext section of the build.gradle file in Listing 1-1 (the top-level build.gradle).

It also declares that we have an "application" with a main class, which will help us run our code after it's written.

Listing 1-3. chapter01-hello-world/build.gradle

```
plugins {
    id "application"
}
dependencies {
    implementation \
    "org.springframework:spring-core:$springFrameworkVersion"
    implementation \
    "org.springframework:spring-context:$springFrameworkVersion"
    implementation \
    "org.springframework:spring-test:$springFrameworkVersion"
}

application {
    mainClass.set("chapter01.Application")
}
```

---

[3] If the references to "depends on" and "versions" are unfamiliar to you, please take a look at the Gradle quickstart; https://docs.gradle.org/current/samples/sample_building_java_applications.html is an excellent resource to provide knowledge you'll need early and often.

It's worth noting here: source code is also going to be complete unless otherwise specified.

In the past, many programming books chose to describe parts of source files, so a given file on disk might be represented in four or five (or more!) source listings in paper.

This means that readers were forced to rely on source code downloads, or their own attention to detail, to see the source files as intended.

Instead, if you see a source file, you're going to see all of it unless it's already been presented, or organization requires otherwise; it's possible that individual methods or sections will be presented before the entire file is shown, but the entire source file will be shown in its entirety.

With that out of the way, it's time to finally see some code!

Our "Hello, World" application will use a Spring component, a "bean," that implements a "message service." This application will be vastly overengineered for what it's designed to do, but it will validate that Spring itself is working in our application.

It will have three parts, the "message service" definition itself, an implementation of that interface, and then an application that uses the interface and its definition.

First, let's take a look at the message service.

Listing 1-4. `chapter01-hello-world/src/main/java/chapter01/MessageService.java`

```
package chapter01;

public interface MessageService {
  public String getMessage();
}
```

This is obviously a very simple interface: it defines a single method, `getMessage()`. Our next class, HelloService, will be just as simple.

Listing 1-5. `chapter01-hello-world/src/main/java/chapter01/HelloService.java`

```
package chapter01;

public class HelloService
  implements MessageService {
  @Override
```

```java
  public String getMessage() {
    return "Hello, world!";
  }
}
```

Lastly, we have the actual application itself.

Let's take a look at the source and then figure out what's going on with it.

Listing 1-6. chapter01-hello-world/src/main/java/
chapter01/Application.java

```java
package chapter01;

import org.springframework.context.annotation.*;

@Configuration
public class Application {

  @Bean
  MessageService helloWorldMessageService() {
    return new HelloService();
  }

  public static void main(String[] args) {
    var context =
      new AnnotationConfigApplicationContext(Application.class);

    var service =
      context.getBean(MessageService.class);
    System.out.println(service.getMessage());
  }
}
```

First, note that we're using a lot of annotations here.

This class is serving both as the entry point for the application and its own configuration: a configuration is annotated with @Configuration.

We're also using a @Bean annotation around a method that returns a MessageService. This annotation declares that the returned value is a component for Spring[4] and gives it a name based on the method used to build the bean, by default: for this bean, it's helloWorldMessageService.

This is how a programmatic configuration marks a component; this allows us to look up components that match a type, which is one of the strongest aspects of Spring.

In main(), we set up an "application context" – a term we're going to use a lot in this book – and then we use the context to look up a MessageService.

Our last action in the code is to write the message to the console.

It's time to run this, because we've put an awful lot of effort into it so far.

If we're in the chapter01-hello-world directory, we can run it with gradle run as seen in Figure 1-4:

```
> gradle run

> Task :chapter01-hello-world:run
Hello, world!

BUILD SUCCESSFUL in 691ms
2 actionable tasks: 1 executed, 1 up-to-date
> []
```

Figure 1-4. Executing the chapter01-hello-world project

As stated before,[5] this code is *massively* overengineered.

But if it runs properly, what we've done is we created an application with a message service component and used that component type to look up an implementation of that service.

Our "application" no longer knows what the component implementation is; it's something that returns a simple, deterministic message, in this case, but could do anything – look up a message from a database or perhaps derive a message from an execution context, for example – and the application would not have to know at all.

---

[4] We will also see other annotations that serve the same role as @Bean in declaring components, with their primary differences being that they mark different *types* of beans, providing programmers with better ideas about how the beans should be used. Other annotations apply actual functional changes as well, but we'll cover those as we get to them.

[5] You *did* read the chapter text exhaustively, didn't you?

That's the true power of Spring: it helps us think in terms of components, which leads us to a process by which we write naturally modular code.

Modular code can be written for testability – a feature we're probably going to lean into here – which means better code.

Hello, Boot

The Spring team released a new mechanism all the way back with Spring 4 called "Spring Boot." Spring Boot (`https://spring.io/projects/spring-boot`) is its own ecosystem by now and provides a very easy and convenient on-ramp to a whole host of features in Spring. It's *so* convenient, in fact, that access to a lot of Spring features nearly mandates the use of Spring Boot; you don't *literally* need it to do many things (after all, it's written with Spring, so if the Spring team can do it, so can you), but many of its features aren't worth replicating outside of Spring Boot.

We'll see a lot of Spring Boot as the book progresses.

To show off a tiny sliver of what it can do, let's write a "Hello World" web service, an application that generates a message when a URL is opened.

The first thing we need to do is configure the build itself. This means creating a directory for the Spring Boot application (`chapter01-hello-boot`), creating a `build.gradle` for the new module, and adding it to our top-level `settings.gradle` file.

Here's our `build.gradle`, which sets up our dependency resolution and a dependency on a `spring-boot-starter-web` module, which imports a lot of features related to cranking up a web service in one easy dependency:

Listing 1-7. `chapter01-hello-boot/build.gradle`

```
plugins {
    id "application"
    id 'org.springframework.boot' version '3.0.0-M4'
    id 'io.spring.dependency-management' version '1.0.13.RELEASE'
}

dependencies {
    implementation \
    'org.springframework.boot:spring-boot-starter-web'
}
```

```
application {
    mainClass.set("chapter01.HelloWorldController")
}
```

This build uses a Spring plug-in for Gradle that allows us to import Spring components from a "bill of materials" – we specify a general name for a dependency, and the plug-in looks up everything we need. Thus, when we include spring-boot-starter-web, the dependency-management plug-in imports a bunch of dependencies for us, so we don't have to worry about looking up specific versions for dependencies.

Next, let's go ahead and fix our settings.gradle, so we can easily compile and run the module. The only line that's changed is the last line.

Listing 1-8. settings.gradle

```
pluginManagement {
    repositories {
        maven {
            url "https://repo.spring.io/milestone"
        }
        maven {
            url "https://repo.spring.io/snapshot"
            mavenContent {
                snapshotsOnly()
            }
        }
        gradlePluginPortal()
    }
}

rootProject.name = 'isf6'
include 'chapter01-hello-world'
include 'chapter01-hello-boot'
```

Now we see that our "book project" has two submodules, one called chapter01-hello-world and the other called chapter01-hello-boot. As we go through the book, we'll need to add each chapter to the settings.gradle.

Lastly, let's look at some Java code.

Listing 1-9. chapter01-hello-boot/src/main/java/chapter01/
HelloWorldController.java

```java
package chapter01;

import org.springframework.boot.SpringApplication;
import org.springframework.boot.autoconfigure.EnableAutoConfiguration;
import org.springframework.stereotype.Controller;
import org.springframework.web.bind.annotation.GetMapping;
import org.springframework.web.bind.annotation.ResponseBody;

@Controller
@EnableAutoConfiguration
public class HelloWorldController {
  @GetMapping(path = "/", produces = "text/plain")
  @ResponseBody
  public String getMessage() {
    return "Hello, world!";
  }

  public static void main(String[] args) {
    SpringApplication.run(HelloWorldController.class,args);
  }
}
```

Here, we're marking the HelloWorldController as a type of component, a @Controller of all things, which means it is meant to handle HTTP requests. We tell it *which* requests with the @GetMapping annotation, telling it to handle requests at the root of the URL – thus, "/" – and that the response content is plain text, and to convert the method's response data directly to the output stream.[6]

Lastly, our main() tells Spring Boot to run with the HelloWorldController as a configurable class. In real practice, this is unwise – we'd normally have a separate "main class" from our controllers (this violates the SOLID principles, as detailed in Chapter 13), but as a trivial example, we're minimizing the number of code listings here.

---

[6] Spring's web services actually have a lot of control over what goes into a response, but our "Hello World" service is very trivial.

We can run this application from Gradle, with `gradle :chapter01-hello-boot:run`. This will output some information on the console, as Spring Boot has logging set up for us by default, and then it will wait for incoming HTTP requests. Our output should look something like Figure 1-5.

Figure 1-5. *Running `gradle :chapter01-hello-boot:run`*

We can see what it generates by hitting `http://localhost:8080/`, which matches the request path set by our `@GetMapping` annotation, and we should see an equivalent for Figure 1-6:

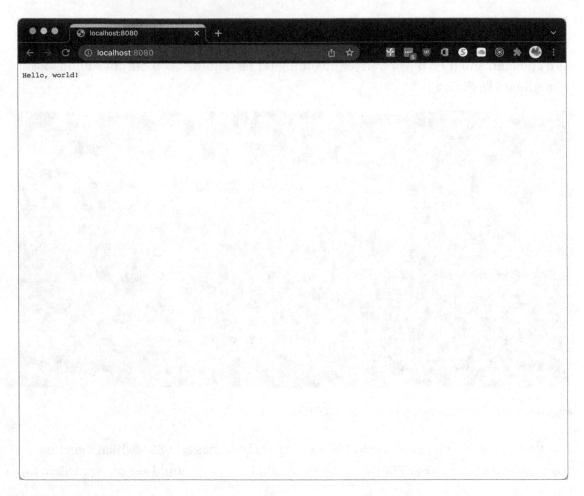

Figure 1-6. *The Response from* `HelloWorldController`

It may not look exciting on the surface, but we've just used Spring Boot to crank up an entire environment for handling HTTP requests, with a few short lines of code.

Hello, Kotlin

Spring Boot will work well with nearly any JVM language, including Groovy, Kotlin, and even Scala. What's more, it works in nearly native fashion for the languages in question. Let's see what that looks like, using Kotlin.[7]

---

[7] Kotlin is a language designed by JetBrains. It can be found at `https://kotlinlang.org/`.

First, we need to add a new module to our `settings.gradle`. This is a single line, as it was with `chapter01-hello-boot` – it should look like this.

Listing 1-10. `settings.gradle`

```
pluginManagement {
    repositories {
        maven {
            url "https://repo.spring.io/milestone"
        }
        maven {
            url "https://repo.spring.io/snapshot"
            mavenContent {
                snapshotsOnly()
            }
        }
        gradlePluginPortal()
    }
}

rootProject.name = 'isf6'
include 'chapter01-hello-world'
include 'chapter01-hello-boot'
include 'chapter01-hello-kotlin'
```

Of course, we need a `build.gradle` – which will look nearly identical to the `build.gradle` in Listing 1-8, with the addition of one line, to add Kotlin compiler support:

Listing 1-11. `chapter01-hello-kotlin/build.gradle`

```
plugins {
    id "application"
    id "org.jetbrains.kotlin.jvm" version "1.7.10"
    id 'org.springframework.boot' version '3.0.0-M4'
    id 'io.spring.dependency-management' version '1.0.13.RELEASE'
}
```

```
dependencies {
    implementation \
    'org.springframework.boot:spring-boot-starter-web'
}

application {
    mainClass.set("chapter01.HelloWorldController")
}
```

Our last file is a direct copy, feature for feature, from Listing 1-9. It has a few differences: namely, it's in src/main/kotlin/chapter01 instead of src/main/java/chapter01 – note the use of kotlin rather than java – and, of course, it's written in Kotlin, with a .kt extension instead of .java. (It also changes the message to "Hello, Kotlin!" to help differentiate it from its Java-based cousin.)

Listing 1-12. chapter01-hello-kotlin/src/main/kotlin/chapter01/HelloWorldController.kt

```kotlin
package chapter01

import org.springframework.boot.SpringApplication
import org.springframework.boot.autoconfigure.EnableAutoConfiguration
import org.springframework.stereotype.Controller
import org.springframework.web.bind.annotation.GetMapping
import org.springframework.web.bind.annotation.ResponseBody

@Controller
@EnableAutoConfiguration
class HelloWorldController {
  @get:ResponseBody
  @get:GetMapping(path = ["/"], produces = ["text/plain"])
  val message: String
    get() = "Hello, Kotlin!"

  companion object {
    @JvmStatic
    fun main(args: Array<String>) {
```

```
    SpringApplication.run(HelloWorldController::class.java, *args)
  }
 }
}
```

You can run *this* class with `gradle :chapter01-hello-kotlin:run`, and opening `http://localhost:8080` now shows a friendly `Hello, Kotlin!` instead of `Hello, world!`

Summary

In this chapter, you saw how to create a simple Spring "Hello World" application and run it. You also learned how Spring uses dependency injection to create all the dependencies and collaboration between classes. Thanks to the small example, you saw that it doesn't matter what implementation you create; as long as you follow the interface, Spring will inject its implementation and have it ready when you need it.

You got a small sneak peek of the Spring Boot, a project by the Spring Team that will be covered in the following chapters. Along the way we got to see how Spring can be used by Kotlin just as easy as it can be used from Java.

The following chapters will cover more detail of the Spring Framework, its features, and its Extensions. You'll learn how they work together and how they can be used in your daily development.

CHAPTER 2

Working with Classes and Dependencies

In this chapter, we're going to see the beginnings of an application to help us maintain references to documents. First, we'll discuss what we're trying to accomplish, and then we'll create classes that can help us keep track of documents; then we'll *use* these classes in a straightforward Java test, and finally, we'll create an equivalent with Spring to demonstrate some more of the framework's capabilities.

The "My Documents" Application

Our application, tentatively named "My Documents" because "Bob" was already taken, is a simple interface where we will eventually be able to add documents of various types – URLs, Word documents, PDFs – for future retrieval.

Our basic requirements for design include the following elements:

1. User authentication (username, password).

2. Ability to add, remove, delete, edit. items/documents like:

    a. Microsoft Office, Apple, Open Documents, and PDF files

    b. Notes (text notes, limited to 255 characters)

    c. Website links (URLs)

3. Every item/document can be private or public.

    a. Private: The owner of the item/documents can see it.

    b. Public: Everybody can see the document.

© Felipe Gutierrez, Joseph B. Ottinger 2022
F. Gutierrez and J. B. Ottinger, *Introducing Spring Framework 6*, https://doi.org/10.1007/978-1-4842-8637-1_2

4. Searchable by keyword, name, type, content, tags, and category.

5. Organizable by category.

6. Every item/document can be sent by email or external messaging system.

However, we're not going to get there in *this* chapter – this chapter is going to introduce some of the beginnings of a system design, through the creation of a SearchEngine that allows us to retrieve documents by type.

We're going to keep expanding the application design through the whole book, adding features as we go, until we've delivered on the entire set of requirements.

Looking over our requirements, we have three entities that stand out for this chapter's scope:

1. Document

2. Document type (which we'll constrain to a few different types, making it a candidate for Java's Enum type)

3. Search engine

Speaking literally, we don't really have a SearchEngine; we have a StorageEngine, but we're going to use SearchEngine here because we're not prepared to add dynamic storage yet.

In fact, that leads us to a fourth type, a StaticSearchEngine, that fulfills the SearchEngine interface while being read-only and presenting only static information.

It's time for us to start writing some of this stuff, to get a feel for how solid the design might be.[1]

First, we need to add a chapter02 directory, along with a build.gradle for it, and we also need to add it to the book's settings.gradle as we did with chapter01-hello-kotlin, and so forth.

Here's the chapter02/build.gradle, which *only* includes the Spring Framework dependencies:

---

[1] The design isn't very solid at all, at this point. It's workable for this chapter's scope, and it can deliver a "viable project" if you're willing to accept static datasets.

Listing 2-1. `chapter02/build.gradle`

```
dependencies {
    implementation \
     "org.springframework:spring-core:$springFrameworkVersion"
    implementation \
     "org.springframework:spring-context:$springFrameworkVersion"
    implementation \
     "org.springframework:spring-test:$springFrameworkVersion"
}
```

We don't have an "application" for this chapter – only a simple implementation of a service that we can expose later – so there's no reference to a main class or an application here. We *only* need the Spring Framework.

We also made a reference to Document and DocumentType. A document has a document type, so let's start with the DocumentType as it is potentially simpler.

We have a few document types we know of, offhand: Word documents, PDFs, notes, and URLs.

DocumentType feels like a good candidate for an enum or a set of Java record types. It turns out Java enum types and records *can* work together, but not especially cleanly, and in this case the overlap is so strong that we really don't get anything from using record – so we'll start off by designing DocumentType as an enum.

Listing 2-2. `chapter02/src/main/java/chapter02/model/DocumentType.java`

```java
package chapter02.model;

public enum DocumentType {
  PDF("PDF", "Portable Document Format", ".pdf"),
  DOCX("DOCX", "Word Document", ".docx"),
  URL("URL", "Universal Resource Locator", ""),
  DOC("DOC", "Word Document", ".doc"),
  NOTE("NOTE", "Ancillary note", "");

  public final String name;
  public final String desc;
  public final String extension;
```

```java
  private DocumentType(String name, String desc, String extension) {
    this.name=name;
    this.desc=desc;
    this.extension=extension;
  }
}
```

We use public final reference values, because String is immutable, and once these objects are instantiated, they will never change.

Next, let's take a look at Document, which is a little longer, thanks to having accessors and one mutator.[2]

Listing 2-3. chapter02/src/main/java/chapter02/model/Document.java

```java
package chapter02.model;

import java.time.LocalDate;
import java.util.StringJoiner;

public class Document {
  private final String name;
  private final DocumentType type;
  private final String location;
  private final LocalDate created;
  private LocalDate modified;

  public Document(String name, DocumentType type, String location) {
    this.name = name;
    this.type = type;
    this.location = location;
    created = LocalDate.now();
    modified = LocalDate.now();
  }
```

---

[2] Your humble author uses "accessor" instead of the more common "getter" and "mutators" to refer to "setters," because ... because... I'm not sure why offhand. You should refer to them however you prefer, and people are likely to know what you're referring to, but this book will refer to accessors and mutators.

```java
public String getName() {
  return name;
}

public DocumentType getType() {
  return type;
}

public String getLocation() {
  return location;
}

public LocalDate getCreated() {
  return created;
}

public LocalDate getModified() {
  return modified;
}

public void setModified(LocalDate modified) {
  this.modified = modified;
}

public String toString() {
  return String.format(
    "%s[name=%s,type=%s,location=%s,created=%tD,modified=%tD]",
    this.getClass().getName(),
    name,
    type,
    location,
    created,
    modified
  );
}
}
```

Our implementation here is very straightforward. We provide accessors for all of our fields, including the final fields, for consistency's sake.

Do you think that DocumentType should follow the same access model, with getName() and so forth, that Document does? Word and line counts were the actual primary motivator for using the different models in this chapter; the shortest method that provided consistency was the approach chosen.

Now we have a way to represent documents with some clarity, although there's still a lot to be desired in terms of being able to search by content. We need two more source files – SearchEngine and StaticSearchEngine – with StaticSearchEngine being something that allows us to test out the interface some.

First, let's take a look at SearchEngine.

Listing 2-4. chapter02/src/main/java/chapter02/service/ SearchEngine.java

```java
package chapter02.service;

import chapter02.model.Document;
import chapter02.model.DocumentType;

import java.util.List;

public interface SearchEngine {
  List<Document> findByType(DocumentType documentType);

  List<Document> listAll();
}
```

Testing the Implementation

Careful readers will notice that we have the beginnings of an object model, something that can represent at least a workable part of our requirements, and we have an interface that can serve as the start of an API to work with that object model.

We have nothing that actually *does* anything, however. It's time to fix that, by writing some tests.

Tests address concerns in two domains: the computational domain and the human domain.

The computational domain is the domain of requirements and function. We want the classes to be able to do *this* and *that*, with *this other* result; tests can verify that this is the case or at least help us identify when it is *not* the case.

The human domain is, well, humans. The human domain of tests allows the demonstration of how an API actually fits into how people should *think about* the API. Are the method names clear and suitable for the task they perform? Does the API require internal knowledge of its workings in order to make sense of things?

Warning   Designing for humans is a very important aspect of API design. Consider JavaMail, for example, which we'll see more in Chapter 11; it's a very powerful library and represents its problem domain very well from a *computational* standpoint. Using it, however, requires an understanding of how SMTP works at the protocol level or how the different mailbox providers operate. It's a good API from a computational domain, but an insufficient one from a human domain; humans should use APIs like Spring Email instead.

It's usually far easier to design an API for other people if you design your tests early in the implementation process. They'll not compile, of course, until you finish writing all of the things your tests require (such as object models, interfaces, and so forth), but writing the tests first often gives you a better idea of what your design actually *needs* and what is most important to design well.

Let's start by looking at a simple, straightforward Java test (with no Spring) to see how our object model might work.

Warning   This test won't run until we have written `StaticSearchEngine` to implement the `SearchEngine` interface. It's shown in the *next* listing.

This is a test, of course, but note the file location. It's in the `src/test/java` tree in chapter02.

Listing 2-5. chapter02/src/test/java/chapter02/MyDocumentsTest.java

```
package chapter02;

import chapter02.service.SearchEngine;
import org.testng.annotations.Test;

import static chapter02.model.DocumentType.PDF;
import static org.testng.Assert.assertEquals;
import static org.testng.Assert.assertNotNull;
```

```java
public class MyDocumentsTest {
  SearchEngine engine = new StaticSearchEngine();

  @Test
  public void testFindByType() {
    var documents = engine.findByType(PDF);
    assertNotNull(documents);
    assertEquals(documents.size(), 1);
    assertEquals(PDF.name,
      documents.get(0).getType().name);
    assertEquals(PDF.desc,
      documents.get(0).getType().desc);
    assertEquals(PDF.extension,
      documents.get(0).getType().extension);
  }

  @Test
  public void testListAll() {
    var documents = engine.listAll();
    assertNotNull(documents);
    assertEquals(documents.size(), 4);
  }

}
```

As a test, it seems fairly sufficient; it relies on some assumptions about the
SearchEngine (it has a single PDF in its data and four total documents), but given those
assumptions, it is fairly complete.[3]

As noted, though, we need an *implementation* of SearchEngine. As you can see
in Listing 2-6, we've named it StaticSearchEngine – meaning that it represents
static data only and is thus completely and utterly predictable. Let's take a look at this
implementation, noting that it, too, is a class meant for testing and thus is in the src/
test/java tree.

---

[3] MyDocumentsTest can be made *more* complete, but then the source listing gets really long. Feel
free to expand!

Listing 2-6. chapter02/src/test/java/chapter02/StaticSearchEngine.java

```java
package chapter02;

import chapter02.model.Document;
import chapter02.model.DocumentType;
import chapter02.service.SearchEngine;

import java.util.List;
import java.util.stream.Collectors;

import static chapter02.model.DocumentType.*;

public class StaticSearchEngine implements SearchEngine {
  private final List<Document> data = populate();

  private List<Document> populate() {
    return List.of(
      new Document(
        "Book Template.pdf", PDF, "/Docs/Template.pdf"
      ),
      new Document(
        "Apress Home Page", URL, "https://apress.com/"
      ),
      new Document(
        "Chapter Template.doc", DOC, "/Docs/Chapter Sample.doc"
      ),
      new Document(
        "Chapter 01.docx", DOCX, "/Docs/Chapter 01.docx"
      )
    );
  }

  @Override
  public List<Document> findByType(DocumentType documentType) {
    return data
      .stream()
      .filter(e -> e.getType().equals(documentType))
      .collect(Collectors.toList());
  }
```

```
@Override
public List<Document> listAll() {
  return data;
}
}
```

This class is not particularly exciting; most of its source is dedicated to creating a known dataset. (We could have stored it externally and loaded it via CSV or some other mechanism like that – even JSON – but loading it would have taken just as much room in this listing.)

We can run this test from Gradle, of course: `gradle :chapter02:test` will compile our source and execute our test, giving us a handy error report if something goes wrong. (Unfortunately, Gradle output for the test run is amazingly bland and just reports success or failure, with a file reference if there's a failure; there's nothing to show readers in terms of Gradle output if we've done our job properly.)

Testing with Spring

Astute readers will note that the book is titled Introducing Spring 6, and we have no Spring in this chapter yet! Time to fix that, and this will show us some of the advantages of using Spring.

Spring is, at its heart, a *dependency injection* library. In our test, we're going to reuse everything we've written, but we're going to use an external configuration to find our SearchEngine implementation.

Using the external configuration for finding resources feels like a very minor thing, but it isn't. It makes our test *modular*. If we had a different implementation of SearchEngine, even if it needed extensive configuration, that configuration can take place in the context of the configuration, as opposed to our test code, and our test could be reused for *any* implementation of SearchEngine as long as the data didn't violate the test's expectations.

Let's take a look at the test itself, which is very nearly identical to Listing 2-5.

Listing 2-7. chapter02/src/test/java/chapter02/MyDocumentsSpringTest.java

```java
package chapter02;

import chapter02.service.SearchEngine;
import org.springframework.beans.factory.annotation.Autowired;
import org.springframework.test.context.ContextConfiguration;
import org.springframework.test.context.testng.AbstractTestNGSpringContextTests;
import org.testng.annotations.Test;

import static chapter02.model.DocumentType.PDF;
import static org.testng.Assert.*;

@ContextConfiguration(classes={TestConfiguration.class})
public class MyDocumentsSpringTest
  extends AbstractTestNGSpringContextTests {

  @Autowired
  SearchEngine engine;

  @Test
  public void testFindByType() {
    var documents = engine.findByType(PDF);
    assertNotNull(documents);
    assertEquals(documents.size(), 1);
    assertEquals(PDF.name,
      documents.get(0).getType().name);
    assertEquals(PDF.desc,
      documents.get(0).getType().desc);
    assertEquals(PDF.extension,
      documents.get(0).getType().extension);
  }

  @Test
  public void testListAll() {
    var documents = engine.listAll();
```

```
    assertNotNull(documents);
    assertEquals(documents.size(),4);
  }
}
```

It has a few differences, though, and they have a lot of impact.

For one thing, the test extends `AbstractTestNGSpringContextTests`, a class that provides some Spring features useful in testing.

Another change is that the test class itself is annotated with a `@ContextConfiguration`:

```
@ContextConfiguration(classes={TestConfiguration.class})
```

This specifies that we're using *programmatic configuration* – a Java class that handles configuration just as we did in our "Hello World" applications from Chapter 1 – and which class name to load for configuration.

Lastly, we have a `SearchEngine` declaration that's annotated with `@Autowired`:

```
@Autowired
SearchEngine engine;
```

Assuming the instance of the test is *managed by Spring*, which it will be given that we've marked it as extending `AbstractTestNGSpringContextTests.` We don't have to use TestNG, of course. JUnit works as well and is quite popular, but we will end up using features that JUnit sees as extensions, and TestNG tends to be a little more straightforward for most common uses, in your author's opinion. `@Autowired` will look for a class instance that fulfills the type requirements in the available configuration and *injects* that reference.

The `AbstractTestNGSpringContextTests` superclass makes this test "managed by Spring," so what Spring is doing is

1. Loading the configuration

2. Loading the test itself

3. Looking for a configuration element that can be assigned to `SearchEngine`

4. Assigning that element's reference to the `engine` attribute

5. Running the tests

After that, the actual tests themselves are boring copies of the tests from MyDocumentsTest.

That leaves the configuration itself, of course, so let's take a look at that.

Listing 2-8. `chapter02/src/test/java/chapter02/TestConfiguration.java`

```java
package chapter02;

import chapter02.service.SearchEngine;
import org.springframework.context.annotation.Bean;
import org.springframework.context.annotation.Configuration;

@Configuration
public class TestConfiguration {
  @Bean
  SearchEngine getEngine() {
    return new StaticSearchEngine();
  }
}
```

This class is very simple: it marks itself as a @Configuration and then declares a single configuration element (with @Bean) that returns an instance of our StaticSearchEngine.

Summary

In this chapter, you defined your first Spring application, called **My Documents**. This application will evolve over the course of the entire book, so you can experiment and add more features using the Spring Framework and its Extensions.

You saw the differences using plain Java, and you added a Spring flavor to it; the Spring Framework will help you to have a better object-oriented design, applying its dependency injection implementation.

In the next chapters, you will dive deeper into Spring and learn how to enhance your application. You will see how to use collections, how to add some persistence, and how to expose your application on the Web and much more.

CHAPTER 3

Applying Different Configurations

The Spring Framework supports different ways to configure its container, and this chapter will cover the XML configuration used previously. Also, you are going to learn how you can accomplish the same configuration using different programmatic mechanisms, which are recommended by the Spring Team.

In the previous chapter, you defined your Spring application, My Documents, and you saw how to use a programmatic configuration file to inject your implementation of the SearchEngine interface. In this chapter, you will be taking a look at the classic XML configuration, which has its own strengths and weaknesses.

Note We're going to be seeing some listings from Chapter 2 again. We're also going to have a *lot* of little listings with a hefty amount of inheritance to avoid rewriting a lot of test code. This chapter is very code-heavy, because it's showing a lot of variants of relatively similar things.

Testing My Documents

We're going to build a series of tests for the "My Documents" application we introduced in Chapter 2. We're not going to add any functionality to the interface, although as we go through this chapter we're going to introduce some new implementations of SearchService.

But first, we need to have the basic model. You can literally copy the source from Chapter 2 into chapter3/src/main/java if you like, but remember to change the package and directory names. As a refresher, here are our three basic types:[1]

Listing 3-1. chapter03/src/main/java/chapter03/model/DocumentType.java

```java
package chapter03.model;

public enum DocumentType {
  PDF("PDF", "Portable Document Format", ".pdf"),
  DOCX("DOCX", "Word Document", ".docx"),
  URL("URL", "Universal Resource Locator", ""),
  DOC("DOC", "Word Document", ".doc"),
  NOTE("NOTE", "Ancillary note", "");

  public final String name;
  public final String desc;
  public final String extension;

  private DocumentType(String name, String desc, String extension) {
    this.name=name;
    this.desc=desc;
    this.extension=extension;
  }
}
```

Listing 3-2. chapter03/src/main/java/chapter03/model/Document.java

```java
package chapter03.model;

import java.time.LocalDate;

public class Document {
  private final String name;
  private final DocumentType type;
```

---

[1] If you're wondering why we don't just have a module for these entities, well, that's a good question. The answer is because we're not going to stick with these rudimentary implementations for long. A common module makes sense but would require that we have stable interfaces, and we're not there. In fact, we'll generally use chapter-specific implementations for most of the book.

```java
private final String location;
private final LocalDate created;
private LocalDate modified;

public Document(String name, DocumentType type, String location) {
  this.name = name;
  this.type = type;
  this.location = location;
  created = LocalDate.now();
  modified = LocalDate.now();
}

public String getName() {
  return name;
}

public DocumentType getType() {
  return type;
}

public String getLocation() {
  return location;
}

public LocalDate getCreated() {
  return created;
}

public LocalDate getModified() {
  return modified;
}

public void setModified(LocalDate modified) {
  this.modified = modified;
}

public String toString() {
  return String.format(
    "%s[name=%s,type=%s,location=%s,created=%tD,modified=%tD]",
    this.getClass().getName(),
```

```
        name,
        type,
        location,
        created,
        modified
      );
   }
}
```

Listing 3-3. chapter03/src/main/java/chapter03/service/SearchEngine.java

```java
package chapter03.service;

import chapter03.model.Document;
import chapter03.model.DocumentType;

import java.util.List;

public interface SearchEngine {
  List<Document> findByType(DocumentType documentType);

  List<Document> listAll();
}
```

Now we get to more fun things. We actually need a hierarchy of tests, and we're also going to need to play with inheritance trees just a touch, because of Java's inheritance scheme.

We're going to have two general *classes* of tests: one class is going to be a pure Java test (as we saw in Chapter 1), and the other class is based on Spring.

However, with TestNG, tests have to inherit from AbstractTestNGSpringContextTests or contend with managing their own Spring contexts. Managing Spring contexts isn't difficult, but it's not really *normal*, and we don't need to practice using things we aren't going to encounter in real code; inheriting from AbstractTestNGSpringContextTests is the "right way to go."

With that said, however, Java only allows *one* superclass, so we can't inherit from a common base test class *and* a Spring test class... or can we?

We can't inherit from two classes, but we *can* inherit from however many interfaces we like, and Java introduced *default implementations* for interfaces all the way back in Java 8. We can make a "base test" interface, and our tests can all implement *that* interface and get the testing methods' implementations.

Let's take a look at our MyDocsBaseTest as a starting point.

Listing 3-4. chapter03/src/test/java/chapter03/MyDocsBaseTest.java

```java
package chapter03;

import chapter03.service.SearchEngine;
import org.testng.annotations.Test;

import static chapter03.model.DocumentType.PDF;
import static org.testng.Assert.assertEquals;
import static org.testng.Assert.assertNotNull;

public interface MyDocsBaseTest {
  SearchEngine getEngine();

  @Test
  default void testEngineNonNull() {
    assertNotNull(getEngine());
  }

  @Test
  default void testFindByType() {
    var documents = getEngine().findByType(PDF);
    assertNotNull(documents);
    assertEquals(documents.size(), 1);
    assertEquals(PDF.name,
      documents.get(0).getType().name);
    assertEquals(PDF.desc,
      documents.get(0).getType().desc);
    assertEquals(PDF.extension,
      documents.get(0).getType().extension);
  }
```

```
@Test
default void testListAll() {
  var documents = getEngine().listAll();
  assertNotNull(documents);
  assertEquals(documents.size(), 4);
}

}
```

The methods themselves are nearly exact copies of the tests we saw in Chapter 2. They are marked as default so that classes that implement this interface get the method bodies automatically, and you'll note that there's a getEngine() call that has no body at all – at some point, our tests are going to need to provide a way to get a SearchEngine.

Before we implement any tests, though, we need an implementation of a SearchEngine again. Let's start with a near-copy of StaticSearchEngine from Chapter 2:

Listing 3-5. chapter03/src/test/java/chapter03/StaticSearchEngine.java

```
package chapter03;

import chapter03.model.Document;
import chapter03.model.DocumentType;
import chapter03.service.SearchEngine;

import java.util.List;
import java.util.stream.Collectors;

import static chapter03.model.DocumentType.*;

public class StaticSearchEngine implements SearchEngine {
  private List<Document> data;

  public StaticSearchEngine(boolean populate) {
    if (populate) {
      populateData();
    }
  }

  public StaticSearchEngine(List<Document> documents) {
    populateData(documents);
  }
```

```java
  public StaticSearchEngine() {
    this(false);
  }

  public void populateData(List<Document> documents) {
    this.data = documents;
  }

  public void populateData() {
    populateData(List.of(
      new Document(
        "Book Template.pdf", PDF, "/Docs/Template.pdf"
      ),
      new Document(
        "Apress Home Page", URL, "https://apress.com/"
      ),
      new Document(
        "Chapter Template.doc", DOC, "/Docs/Chapter Sample.doc"
      ),
      new Document(
        "Chapter 01.docx", DOCX, "/Docs/Chapter 01.docx"
      )
    ));
  }

  @Override
  public List<Document> findByType(DocumentType documentType) {
    return data
      .stream()
      .filter(e -> e.getType().equals(documentType))
      .collect(Collectors.toList());
  }

  @Override
  public List<Document> listAll() {
    return data;
  }
}
```

There are a number of fairly subtle changes to this class, mostly around populating the data. In Chapter 2, we populated the data at class instantiation, whereas here we call populateData() optionally during construction. By default, we do *not* populate data; thus, we'll need to pass true to the secondary constructor to initiate setting up our dataset when we get to writing the tests in Listing 3-6. We also have a populateData() that takes a List<Document>.

Note   We're going to have some examples where we explicitly populate the data later in this chapter. As a result, this class now has some features that don't make sense for what we've displayed so far.

Let's build a test that doesn't use Spring at all. MyDocsJavaTest will be a feature-for-feature replacement for the test we saw in Listing 2-5, but thanks to the interface, it's far shorter, focusing *only* on building a SearchEngine.

Warning   Note that MyDocsJavaTest uses a @Test annotation on the *class*! This is because it has no tests in and of itself, so we need to tell TestNG to include the class in its list of tests.

Listing 3-6. chapter03/src/test/java/chapter03/MyDocsJavaTest.java

```java
package chapter03;

import chapter03.service.SearchEngine;
import org.testng.annotations.Test;

@Test
public class MyDocsJavaTest
  implements MyDocsBaseTest {
  SearchEngine engine = new StaticSearchEngine(true);

  @Override
  public SearchEngine getEngine() {
    return engine;
  }
}
```

As we saw in Chapter 2, we can run the test with `gradle :chapter03:test`, which will compile the source code and run every test in the chapter project.

What we see here is a demonstration of the basic responsibility of every one of our other test classes: a way to fulfill `getEngine()`. Here, we do it statically, as you can see. The test creates a `StaticSearchEngine` (with populated data!) and returns it.

The Spring tests will do the same thing, except they'll let Spring populate the engine, and our tests will differ only in how they specify *where* and *how* to load the Spring configuration.

Annotation Configuration in Spring

Programmatic configuration via annotations is *generally* preferred by the majority of Spring developers.[2]

With one version of annotation configuration – programmatic configuration, or Java configuration – you create classes that are marked with the `@Configuration` annotation, and then mark accessors within those classes with `@Bean`, among a few other candidates.

Note   @Bean is not the only annotation that provides a Spring bean. We will explore others as we progress through this book. In fact, we'll take a look at some of them later in this chapter.

We saw this form of programmatic configuration in Listing 3-7. We can represent that here with a single `.java` source file, with two classes contained in it.

Listing 3-7. `chapter03/src/test/java/chapter03/MyDocsConfigurationTest.java`

```
package chapter03;

import chapter03.service.SearchEngine;
import org.springframework.beans.factory.annotation.Autowired;
import org.springframework.context.annotation.Bean;
import org.springframework.context.annotation.Configuration;
```

---

[2] Anecdotal data about preferences provided by the Spring Team itself and has no bearing on which configuration method is best for a given application. Each mechanism has its own strengths and weaknesses.

```java
import org.springframework.test.context.ContextConfiguration;
import org.testng.annotations.Test;

@Configuration
class MyDocsConfig {
  @Bean
  SearchEngine getEngineBean() {
    return new StaticSearchEngine(true);
  }
}

@ContextConfiguration(classes={MyDocsConfig.class})
@Test
public class MyDocsConfigurationTest
  extends MyDocsContextBaseTest {
  @Autowired
  SearchEngine engine;

  @Override
  public SearchEngine getEngine() {
    return engine;
  }
}
```

Note   Remember, Java can only have one top-level `public` class in a given source file but can contain other *nonpublic* classes in the source.

As we see here, we have a field marked as `@Autowired` that Spring will automatically supply as part of the test's lifecycle, thanks to the `MyDocsConfig` class having a method marked with `@Bean` that returns a type that is *assignable to* the autowired field. The accessor merely provides access to the attribute, and our inherited tests run properly as expected.

Another thing to note here is the *naming* of the component. In Chapter 1, we saw a component returned from a method called `helloWorldMessageService()`, which was used as the name for the component; here, Spring will assign a name of `engineBean` and not getEngineBean, deriving the name from the method such that it makes sense to humans as best it can. We could, of course, also give the component a name, with @Bean(name="beanName") to give it an arbitrary name.[3]

Component Scanning

The other aspect of annotation-based configuration relies on *component scanning*. In a configuration class, we use annotations like @Bean to mark methods that are bean providers *in that class*, but we're not limited to using @Bean on methods in a Java configuration. We can also mark classes themselves as Spring components and tell Spring to *look for them* in the classpath.

This is an "expensive operation," potentially, because we can ask Spring to search large parts of the classpath; the solution here is to limit the search.

Let's revisit Listing 3-7, except we'll **search** for the SearchEngine by using component scanning instead of declaring it explicitly.

First, we need our SearchEngine implementation, which we'll put into its own package, chapter03.service.

Listing 3-8. chapter03/src/test/java/chapter03/service/Scanned SearchEngine.java

```java
package chapter03.service;

import chapter03.StaticSearchEngine;
import org.springframework.stereotype.Service;

@Service
public class ScannedSearchEngine
  extends StaticSearchEngine {
  ScannedSearchEngine() {
    super(true);
  }
}
```

---

[3] It's worth noting that *generally speaking* using bean names in Spring isn't necessary or encouraged. It would only matter when you have more than one component that was assignable to a single type – if we had multiple SearchEngine implementations in our configuration, for example. Then we could use the name to specify which of the implementations we wanted, when requesting one. With that said, that is usually a fairly rare occurrence in practice.

We annotate this with @Service, much as we've annotated other components with @Bean. @Bean is a method-level annotation; we use it in a programmatic configuration to say "this method returns a component." At the *class* level, we use one of four possible candidates: @Component, @Service, @Repository, or @Controller. All four mark the classes as components, but there are some subtle differences in how they cause Spring to treat the classes.

Annotation	Description
@Component	Generalized annotation that marks the component as a candidate for Spring to manage.
@Repository	This is a specialization of @Component and marks this component as interacting with a data layer of some kind. Exceptions can be translated automatically into Spring's persistence-related exceptions.
@Service	This is a specialization of @Component and marks this component as being a type of service for the application; it's a semantic difference for programmer convenience more than anything else.
@Controller	This is another specialization of @Component and marks the component as being used in a web context.

In ScannedSearchEngine, we have a possible candidate for a @Repository, in that it uses read operations, but architecturally, it would probably have a storage engine that the SearchEngine delegates to, rather than being a repository itself. Therefore we've marked it as a @Service.

Listing 3-9. chapter03/src/test/java/chapter03/MyDocsScanTest.java

```
package chapter03;

import chapter03.service.SearchEngine;
import org.springframework.beans.factory.annotation.Autowired;
import org.springframework.context.annotation.ComponentScan;
import org.springframework.context.annotation.Configuration;
import org.springframework.test.context.ContextConfiguration;
import org.testng.annotations.Test;
```

```
@Configuration
@ComponentScan(basePackages = "chapter03.service")
class MyDocsScanConfig {
}

@ContextConfiguration(classes={MyDocsScanConfig.class})
@Test
public class MyDocsScanTest
  extends MyDocsContextBaseTest {
  @Autowired
  SearchEngine engine;

  @Override
  public SearchEngine getEngine() {
    return engine;
  }
}
```

Here, we have a MyDocsScanConfig class that is marked as a @Configuration, but we also have a @ComponentScan annotation, and we've told *this* annotation to scan the chapter03.service package – otherwise, it will scan all of the packages whose names start with *the configuration class'* package. Thus, since this configuration class is in chapter03, if we didn't pass a basePackages value, the scan would include chapter03 – the current package – and any packages "under" chapter03.[4]

When this test is run, Spring will examine **every** class specified in the @ComponentScan and check to see if it's a @Component or a specialization of a component, like a @Service. If it is, it will load that class into the ApplicationContext and make it available for use, which means the autowiring works for MyDocsScanTest and our tests pass.

Note   In general, the explicit configuration classes we've seen so far are the "lightest" approaches to configuration. Component scanning is convenient, but a bit heavier.

---

[4] Java packages are *not* actually hierarchical in nature; packages aren't "subpackages" of other packages except semantically.

XML Configuration in Spring

Our next class looks almost identical to the MyDocsConfigurationTest class, with two differences. One is that there's no MyDocsConfig class; the other difference is that the @ContextConfiguration is going to refer to an XML configuration instead of a class. Let's take a look at MyDocsXMLTest first, then we'll take a look at the XML itself, and we'll discuss a little why we might use XML for configuration.

Listing 3-10. chapter03/src/test/java/chapter03/MyDocsXMLTest.java

```
package chapter03;

import chapter03.service.SearchEngine;
import org.springframework.beans.factory.annotation.Autowired;
import org.springframework.test.context.ContextConfiguration;
import org.testng.annotations.Test;

@ContextConfiguration(locations={"/documents.xml"})
@Test
public class MyDocsXMLTest
  extends MyDocsContextBaseTest {
  @Autowired
  SearchEngine engine;

  @Override
  public SearchEngine getEngine() {
    return engine;
  }
}
```

The @ContextConfiguration annotation uses a locations attribute, which is a collection of named resources on the classpath. Since we refer to /documents.xml, it will load that resource from the root of the classpath. In our project here, it's in chapter03/src/test/resources/documents.xml – which we'll see in our next Listing – so it's available for the test.

Functionally there's nothing unique or special here. Here's the XML configuration, which starts to show us something a little more interesting:

Listing 3-11. `chapter03/src/test/resources/documents.xml`

```xml
<?xml version="1.0" encoding="UTF-8"?>
<beans xmlns="http://www.springframework.org/schema/beans"
       xmlns:xsi="http://www.w3.org/2001/XMLSchema-instance"
       xsi:schemaLocation="http://www.springframework.org/schema/beans
       http://www.springframework.org/schema/beans/spring-beans.xsd">

  <bean id="engine"
        class="chapter03.StaticSearchEngine"
        init-method="populateData"
  />
</beans>
```

Here we see an *awful* lot of text compared to the `MyDocsConfig` class, and hardly any of it is unique to our application; only the `<bean/>` reference has anything to do with our test. What *it* does is fairly simple: it marks a Spring bean (equivalent to the `@Bean` annotation) and gives it a name (`"engine"`), which the annotation *implies* unless you give it a specific name, and then suggests the implementating class, which – just as with our other tests – is `StaticSearchEngine`.

XML is a fairly large, very formal specification. For small configurations like this one, they're very verbose – there's a lot of boilerplate required by XML itself that makes our simple configuration six lines of boilerplate for two lines of actual content – a fairly poor signal-to-noise ratio.[5]

XML starts with a preamble to say that it's an XML file and then has a hierarchical node structure: there's a top-level node (`<beans>`) that describes the content with various *attributes* (the `xmlns`, `xmlns:xsi`, and `xsi:schemaLocation` bits) and then contains more nodes before its end tag, which is the node name prefaced with a slash (thus: `</beans>`).

A node doesn't *have* to contain other nodes, as we see with `<bean>`, which ends itself with a slash before the closing angle bracket.

The attributes on the top node introduce *XML namespaces*, which inform an XML parser what the XML file is supposed to look like. The `xmlns` says that `<beans>` uses a specific schema by default (the `beans` schema, referred to by URL), which itself says

---

[5] Six lines of boilerplate to two lines of content could have been worse, too, because the two lines of content could have been one if we had a wider margin to work with, and even there, we're barely scratching the surface of the boilerplate we *could* have had.

that a <beans> node contains specific other nodes, such as <bean>, and what *those* can or must look like for the XML file to be valid.

As stated, it's a *very* formal specification, and a lot of programmers resent the formality; XML is very, very powerful but not very popular.

Note   Most programmers, including the Spring Team itself, prefer configuration in code rather than with XML, and when XML is used, the files are generated with tools that handle all the namespaces automatically, or the headers are copied from other files.

With that said, though, there *is* a use for the XML format. Before we show some of the more useful aspects of XML configuration, let's figure out what our *current* configuration is doing with that single <bean/> reference.

The <bean> tag can have *many* options. As a short example of some of them:

Attribute	Description
id	An identifier for the bean. Only one unique ID can be defined.
class	Points to a concrete class, given the full Java package.
scope	Tells the Spring container how it will create the bean; by default if this scope property is not set, the bean will be a singleton instance. Other scopes are prototype (an instance is created every time the bean is required), request (a single instance is created in each HTTP web request), and session (a bean is created and lives during the HTTP session).
init-method	This is the name of the method that will be called after a bean is created. It's useful when you want to set a state after your object is created.
factory-method	This is the name of the method that will be used to create the bean. In other words, you need to provide the method that will create the instance of the object, and this method should have parameters.
destroy-method	This is the name of the method that will be called after you dispose of the bean.
lazy-init	This can be set to true if you want the container to create your bean when it's being called or used by you (when you called the getBean method from the ApplicationContext) or maybe later from another instance class that requires your object.

What our simple configuration does, then, is declare a Spring configuration (with all the preamble and XML declaration), and then it creates a single reference, with the identifier of engine, and that its type is chapter03.StaticSearchEngine, and after the class is instantiated, we call populateData(). Since we provide no other tags like scope, it is created as a singleton (every time we ask the context for engine we'll get the *same reference*) and is constructed through the use of a constructor with no arguments (the Java default constructor).

Expanding the Configuration

The problem with our simple configuration is that it is *too* simple. It's also underpowered. Let's fix that a bit.

The chapter03.StaticSearchEngine we've been using is a decent implementation for its purpose; it fulfills the implementation of a SearchEngine with constant data.

However, it's very verbose (because it has to include the constant data), and nobody likes verbose code listings, because they consume a lot of paper, and that uses up a lot of trees, right?[6]

We're going to explore a few different ways to create seed data throughout this book, but let's start here by using our XML configuration to explore a few options. We're going to see a few different sets of code listings, where we provide an XML configuration and then a Java class, so be ready.

First, let's see how we can construct our test such that we don't have to use init-method, by specifying constructor arguments. Here's our test class:

Listing 3-12. chapter03/src/test/java/chapter03/
MyDocsXMLConstructorTest.java

```
package chapter03;

import chapter03.service.SearchEngine;
import org.springframework.beans.factory.annotation.Autowired;
import org.springframework.test.context.ContextConfiguration;
import org.testng.annotations.Test;
```

---

[6] The Lorax fully endorses this message.

```
@ContextConfiguration(locations={"/doccons.xml"})
@Test
public class MyDocsXMLConstructorTest
  extends MyDocsContextBaseTest {
  @Autowired
  SearchEngine engine;

  @Override
  public SearchEngine getEngine() {
    return engine;
  }
}
```

Again, functionally there's nothing unique or special here. Here's the XML configuration, which starts to show us something a little more interesting:

Listing 3-13. chapter03/src/test/resources/doccons.xml

```xml
<?xml version="1.0" encoding="UTF-8"?>
<beans xmlns="http://www.springframework.org/schema/beans"
       xmlns:xsi="http://www.w3.org/2001/XMLSchema-instance"
       xsi:schemaLocation="http://www.springframework.org/schema/beans
       http://www.springframework.org/schema/beans/spring-beans.xsd">

  <bean id="engine"
        class="chapter03.StaticSearchEngine">
    <constructor-arg
        name="populate"
        type="boolean"
        value="true" />
  </bean>
</beans>
```

Here, we see the use of a `constructor-arg` tag inside the bean tag. This allows us to pass constructor arguments, surprisingly enough, and can specify the specific argument by name (as is done here) or by position. The type is required, and we're passing a value as opposed to a reference – which implies that we could have a bean that was a simple boolean value of true, if we'd needed or wanted that.[7]

Note   Compare and contrast this configuration with Listing 3-7 – and you'll see why many programmers prefer the programmatic configuration.

Let's explore more, though, and try to figure out if we can make the XML configuration work for us instead of just being excessively verbose for the job we're asking it to perform. Let's use it to populate our dataset.

Just to get it out of the way, let's take a look at our test source. As with our other Spring tests that use XML configuration, the only real differences here are in the name of the class and the @ContextConfiguration annotation.

Listing 3-14. chapter03/src/test/java/chapter03/MyDocsXMLDataTest.java

```java
package chapter03;

import chapter03.service.SearchEngine;
import org.springframework.beans.factory.annotation.Autowired;
import org.springframework.test.context.ContextConfiguration;
import org.testng.annotations.Test;

@ContextConfiguration(locations={"/docdata.xml"})
@Test
public class MyDocsXMLDataTest
  extends MyDocsContextBaseTest {
  @Autowired
  SearchEngine engine;

  @Override
  public SearchEngine getEngine() {
    return engine;
  }
}
```

---

[7] We will show the use of references soon.

We're going to populate our dataset by using a different tag in our XML configuration, from a different XML *namespace*, the util namespace. This means our XML header is going to change.

Once we've done that, we'll be able to use a list tag, and in the list we will be able to include a series of other values. This is going to be a very verbose XML file, but it will show us a few things: how to construct a list as a value and how to refer to a Spring bean as a reference for a constructor, for example:[8]

Listing 3-15. chapter03/src/test/resources/docdata.xml

```xml
<?xml version="1.0" encoding="UTF-8"?>
<beans xmlns="http://www.springframework.org/schema/beans"
       xmlns:xsi="http://www.w3.org/2001/XMLSchema-instance"
       xmlns:util="http://www.springframework.org/schema/util"
       xsi:schemaLocation="http://www.springframework.org/schema/beans
       http://www.springframework.org/schema/beans/spring-beans.xsd
       http://www.springframework.org/schema/util
       http://www.springframework.org/schema/util/spring-util.xsd">

  <bean id="engine"
        class="chapter03.StaticSearchEngine">
   <constructor-arg name="documents" ref="documentList"/>
  </bean>

  <util:list id="documentList"
             value-type="chapter03.model.Document">
   <bean id="doc1" class="chapter03.model.Document">
    <constructor-arg
        name="name"
        value="Book Template.pdf"/>
    <constructor-arg
        name="type"
        value="PDF"/>
```

---

[8] The dataset construction will also inspire us to find easier ways to load data from an external source. The XML is very simple but is very verbose for what it gives us.

```xml
    <constructor-arg
        name="location"
        value="/Docs/Template.pdf"/>
</bean>
<bean id="doc2" class="chapter03.model.Document">
  <constructor-arg
      name="name"
      value="Apress Home Page"/>
  <constructor-arg
      name="type"
      value="URL"/>
  <constructor-arg
      name="location"
      value="https://apress.com"/>
</bean>
<bean id="doc3" class="chapter03.model.Document">
  <constructor-arg
      name="name"
      value="Chapter Template.doc"/>
  <constructor-arg
      name="type"
      value="DOC"/>
  <constructor-arg
      name="location"
      value="/Docs/Chapter Sample.doc"/>
</bean>
<bean id="doc4" class="chapter03.model.Document">
  <constructor-arg
      name="name"
      value="Chapter 01.docx"/>
  <constructor-arg
      name="type"
      value="DOCX"/>
  <constructor-arg
      name="location"
```

```
        value="/Docs/Chapter 01.docx"/>
    </bean>
  </util:list>
</beans>
```

The MyDocsXMLDataTest tests run successfully given this configuration, which tells us the list is being populated with the right number of elements (our test doesn't validate the entire list, after all, although that might be a good exercise for the reader) and that it has at least one of the correct elements in the list.

Component Scanning in XML

We saw earlier in this chapter that we could scan for components in Java instead of having to declare them explicitly. We can do the same in XML, using a *different* namespace, the context namespace, much as we use the util namespace. Our configuration for component scanning might look like this:

Listing 3-16. chapter03/src/test/resources/docscan.xml

```
<?xml version="1.0" encoding="UTF-8"?>
<beans xmlns="http://www.springframework.org/schema/beans"
       xmlns:xsi="http://www.w3.org/2001/XMLSchema-instance"
       xmlns:context="http://www.springframework.org/schema/context"
       xsi:schemaLocation="http://www.springframework.org/schema/beans
       http://www.springframework.org/schema/beans/spring-beans.xsd
       http://www.springframework.org/schema/context
       https://www.springframework.org/schema/context/spring-context.xsd">

  <context:component-scan base-package="chapter03.service" />
</beans>
```

This configuration is a drop-in replacement for the component-scanning configuration we saw in Listing 3-9. The key is the inclusion of the context namespace, which provides the component-scan tag.

Note that we are not *using* this configuration yet – let's consider the value of all this XML, and then we'll see this configuration in use in Listing 3-17 just to prove it works as intended.

Is XML Configuration a Good Idea?

If the question is "Is XML configuration a good idea," the answer has to be "yes," but with a caveat: "when?"

Unfortunately, answering **when** XML configuration is a good idea is a little harder. Here, we've had a separate test class for **each** of our XML configurations, so there's a lot of repetition: we *could* have had a single test class and provided it a list of XML configurations, which would allow us to rapidly test each configuration in order.

If we shorten one of the tests, it might look something like this:

Listing 3-17. chapter03/src/test/java/chapter03/MyDocsAllXMLsTest.java

```
package chapter03;

import chapter03.service.SearchEngine;
import org.springframework.context.support.ClassPathXmlApplicationContext;
import org.testng.annotations.DataProvider;
import org.testng.annotations.Test;

import static chapter03.model.DocumentType.PDF;
import static org.testng.Assert.assertEquals;
import static org.testng.Assert.assertNotNull;

public class MyDocsAllXMLsTest {
  @DataProvider
  Object[][] getConfigs() {
    return new Object[][]{
      new Object[]{"classpath:/documents.xml"},
      new Object[]{"classpath:/doccons.xml"},
      new Object[]{"classpath:/docdata.xml"},
      new Object[]{"classpath:/docscan.xml"}};
  }

  @Test(dataProvider = "getConfigs")
  public void testSpring(String configLocation) {
    var context=
      new ClassPathXmlApplicationContext(configLocation);
```

```
    var engine=context.getBean(SearchEngine.class);
    assertNotNull(engine);
    assertEquals(engine.listAll().size(), 4);
    assertEquals(
      engine.findByType(PDF).get(0).getName(),
      "Book Template.pdf");
  }
}
```

This uses TestNG's @DataProvider annotation to feed each XML configuration name into a single method, which itself applies each of the tests (or an equivalent of them) from MyDocsBaseTest. It isn't quite an exact equivalent, because the MyDocsBaseTest class is designed around having sole access to a SearchEngine, but it demonstrates dynamically loading each XML file in rapid order; this **can** be done without using XML, but in such cases XML is fairly convenient.

With that said, though, we've designed our configurations in such a way that XML configuration works fairly naturally (thanks to our use of static data in StaticSearchEngine) and environments with more complete features would see diminishing returns for the effort expended.

In general, as a programmer, you'll find yourself gravitating toward programmatic configuration, which feels far more natural as well as being far less verbose than the XML equivalents.

Choosing a Configuration Approach

We've seen two different ways to approach configuration in Spring: programmatic configuration with a Java class and XML. We've seen component scanning as a variant for both Java and XML as well, which can be considered a third way to configure your components.

Type of Configuration	Usage
XML	This can be used with third-party libraries and/or different development environments. It's generally easy to read and follow, but it is very verbose and configurations need to be individually tracked.[9]
Annotations	It is another way to do configurations, but here you are attaching the Spring context to your application (i.e., you're adding a Spring annotation at the *source level* to your components, and thus Spring must be in the compilation classpath for you to compile your classes; if your application uses Spring, of course, this is a very minor problem).
Java Bean Configuration	This is the generally preferred mechanism for configuration, as developers are used to compilation; it's very easy to understand and can also be very explicit.

Summary

In this chapter, we saw multiple different ways to load a Spring configuration – programmatic configuration, with component scanning as an alternative, and declarative configuration with XML, also with component scanning as a possibility.

In the next chapter, we're going to start adding features to our application.

---

[9] One of the neat features of XML configuration is that you can import one configuration file into another, a feature we did not demonstrate here because our configuration was too simple. In practice, this is done with third-party integrations, but *also* such integrations usually rely on component scanning or programmatic configuration.

CHAPTER 4

Using Bean Scopes

So far, we've seen the basic requirements of a **My Documents** application, and we've explored some aspects of configuration of a simple implementation of a search engine that can return either *all* documents or documents of a specific type.

In all cases, we've returned what is effectively a *singleton* of every implementation, meaning that Spring constructs *one* instance of each component.

In this chapter, we're going to spend some time with bean *scopes*, which control when Spring constructs objects and how it uses them.

Scope

Scope is a term used in programming to describe *visibility*. In a programming language, a reference is "in scope" when it's accessible; in Java, a reference can't be used from outside a function if it's declared *in* a function (unless, of course, it's returned or exposed somehow).

It also refers to the *lifecycle* of a reference, which is how Spring refers to it.

The Scopes

Spring actually has *six* scopes available,[1] with four of them being applicable only in a web application's context, which means that we'll have to read more about them later – although we can take the concepts we'll learn in *this* chapter and apply them when we encounter web applications in more depth.

---

[1] There is actually another bean scope *available*, called thread, but you have to do some setup to use it. It's not typically registered because scoping a bean to a thread tends to create memory leaks unless the programmer is very careful.

© Felipe Gutierrez, Joseph B. Ottinger 2022
F. Gutierrez and J. B. Ottinger, *Introducing Spring Framework 6*, https://doi.org/10.1007/978-1-4842-8637-1_4

singleton	Scopes a single bean definition to a single object instance per Spring `ApplicationContext`.
prototype	Scopes a single bean definition to any number of object instances.
request	Scopes a single bean definition to the lifecycle of a single HTTP request; that is, each and every HTTP request will have its own instance of a bean created off the back of a single bean definition. Only valid in the context of a web-aware Spring `ApplicationContext`.
session	Scopes a single bean definition to the lifecycle of a HTTP session. Only valid in the context of a web-aware Spring `ApplicationContext`.
global session	Scopes a single bean definition to the lifecycle of a global HTTP session. Typically only valid when used in a portlet context. Only valid in the context of a web-aware Spring `ApplicationContext`.

The two scopes we care about here are `singleton` and `prototype`.

A singleton, in Java, normally refers to a single reference that is made widely available – an object that you only need (or want) one of. Java doesn't really support the concept of a *true* singleton – it can be done, but it's absurdly difficult.

Instead, Java supports the idea of a singleton *per classloader*, which has its own difficulties, and because Java is multithreaded by design, even constructing a singleton for a given classloader can be hard to guarantee. Note that it's not *impossible* and once you know what you're doing and accept the limitations, it can be reduced to a simple pattern (to wit: instantiate statically and early).

In Spring, a singleton is scoped to an application context, but within a given application context, any time you retrieve an object, you'll get the same object reference.

A component that is scoped as a *prototype* is constructed *every time you retrieve a matching object from the context*, using the definition as a model. This definition is important: if you retrieve a prototyped component from the context and then pass that component around, you're going to have the same reference; Spring isn't going to reach into your code and create new references for you. You *have* to retrieve them explicitly from the context to trigger the prototyped behavior.

Note   The default scope is `singleton` – if you don't tell Spring explicitly what scope to use, you're going to get the singleton behavior.

Singletons are appropriate when your components don't manage state. If you need to manage object state, such as tracking a status of a given object or conversation, a prototype is best.

Using the Scopes

In order to examine our scopes, we're going to build a `chapter04` project, of course, but we're also going to build a test class that loads XML configurations and run our tests using those configurations. They won't be long, but they'll have some subtle differences, so be careful.

Our `build.gradle` is quite literally a copy of the `build.gradle` from Chapter 3.

Listing 4-1. `chapter04/build.gradle`

```
dependencies {
    implementation  \
     "org.springframework:spring-core:$springFrameworkVersion"
    implementation  \
     "org.springframework:spring-context:$springFrameworkVersion"
    implementation  \
     "org.springframework:spring-test:$springFrameworkVersion"
}
```

We need to add a reference to our top-level `settings.gradle`:

Listing 4-2. `settings.gradle`

```
// prior content in settings.gradle
include 'chapter02'
include 'chapter03'
include 'chapter04'
```

Before we take a look at the test itself, let's see some classes that we'll use to test out our scopes: a `Producer` and `Consumer` class.

The `Producer` produces a value, a number of times a given method is called, and maintains internal state to track this number. (This will be relevant for testing out our bean scopes.) It also helpfully tells us when it's being constructed.

Listing 4-3. chapter04/src/test/java/c04/Producer.java

```java
package c04;

import org.slf4j.Logger;
import org.slf4j.LoggerFactory;

public class Producer {
  Logger logger = LoggerFactory.getLogger(this.getClass());
  int executions = 0;

  Producer() {
    logger.info("constructed as "+Integer.toHexString(hashCode()));
  }

  int execute() {
    return ++executions;
  }
}
```

Next comes our Consumer class, which has no internal state of its own but uses a Producer and tells us what Producer with which it is constructed.

Listing 4-4. chapter04/src/test/java/c04/Consumer.java

```java
package c04;

import org.slf4j.Logger;
import org.slf4j.LoggerFactory;
import org.springframework.context.annotation.Scope;

public class Consumer {
  Logger logger= LoggerFactory.getLogger(this.getClass());

  Producer producer;

  Consumer(Producer producer) {
    this.producer=producer;
    logger.info("constructed with producer "
      +Integer.toHexString(producer.hashCode()));
  }
```

```
  Producer getProducer() {
    return producer;
  }

  int execute() {
    return producer.execute();
  }
}
```

Now we're going to drop into a more complicated test class. What we want to do is have a test class that loads a configuration and then validates what that configuration *does* as part of our test. We'll need some components to test with: a Consumer and a Producer, with the Consumer exposing the Producer to our test, so we can validate the configuration settings and behavior.

Note   We're changing the chapter packages to use c04 instead of the chapter04 we've been using, because chapter is very verbose for repeated use.

Listing 4-5. chapter04/src/test/java/c04/ScopesTest.java

```
package c04;

import org.springframework.context.ApplicationContext;
import org.springframework.context.support.ClassPathXmlApplicationContext;
import org.springframework.core.io.Resource;
import org.springframework.core.io.support.ResourcePatternUtils;
import org.testng.annotations.DataProvider;
import org.testng.annotations.Test;

import java.io.IOException;
import java.util.Arrays;

import static org.testng.Assert.assertEquals;

public class ScopesTest {
  @DataProvider
  public Object[][] getConfigurations() {
    var resolver =
      ResourcePatternUtils.getResourcePatternResolver(null);
```

```java
    try {
      var resourceNames = Arrays
        .stream(resolver.getResources("classpath*:*.xml"))
        .map(Resource::getFilename)
        .map(e -> new String[]{e})
        .toList()
        .toArray(new Object[0][]);
      return resourceNames;
    } catch (IOException e) {
      throw new RuntimeException(e);
    }
  }

  boolean getValue(ApplicationContext context,
                   String name) {
    try {
      return context.getBean(name, Boolean.class);
    } catch (Exception ignored) {
      return false;
    }
  }

  @Test(dataProvider = "getConfigurations")
  public void testConfiguration(String configName) {
    var context =
      new ClassPathXmlApplicationContext(configName);
    var p1 = context.getBean(Producer.class);
    var p2 = context.getBean(Producer.class);
    var c1 = context.getBean(Consumer.class);
    var c2 = context.getBean(Consumer.class);
    var producerPrototype = getValue(context, "producerBean");
    var consumerPrototype = getValue(context, "consumerBean");

    assertEquals(p1 == p2, !producerPrototype);
    assertEquals(c1 == c2, !consumerPrototype);

    // the consumer is the *same reference* if
    // consumerPrototype is true, so the
```

```
  // producerPrototype is not used more than once.
  assertEquals(c1.getProducer() == c2.getProducer(),
    !(producerPrototype && consumerPrototype));
  // if producerPrototype is true, then the sequence will fail
  assertEquals((p1.execute() + 1) == p2.execute(), !producerPrototype);
  }
}
```

There are a number of things going on here. The intent of this class is to iterate through a number of configurations, applying the same tests to every configuration.

But the configurations specify different things, so we're going to try to include information about *expected values* from the configurations, too.

As a result, our test has three components: the first is a data provider method that uses a ResourcePatternResolver (acquired from ResourcePatternUtils) to scan the classpath for our configurations. It returns those matching resources as Resource references in a flat array, so we have to convert it into an Object[][] containing only the filenames. The pattern ("classpath*:*.xml") will match *every XML file* in our classpath.

The second component is a method to pull a boolean value out of a configuration. It provides us the convenience of assuming a value is false unless otherwise specified.

The third method is the interesting one. It receives a configuration name (via the data provider, getConfigurations()), loads the configuration, and then gets *four* beans references: two Producer references and two Consumer references.

It *also* gets two boolean values – which default to false, thanks to our getValue() method – that indicate whether the configuration has set the scope of a given type to prototype or not.[2]

If the type is set to prototype, then the two references will *not be the same reference*. They may have the same values – and should, realistically – but the actual references will be different.

The third assertEquals is a little confusing, though. There's actually a matrix of possibilities: we only use prototype when a type is *actively requested* from the context, so we can have a Consumer prototype that gets given the same Producer instance over and over again – i.e., unique Consumer and common Producer – or we can have a

---

[2] We could have read the configuration manually and looked for the scope attribute directly; there are also ways to look at the application context and figure out the scope from its internal data structures. This was simpler and avoided the distraction of walking through extra code.

Producer prototype, but a singleton `Consumer,` so when that *one* consumer is created, it gets a unique `Producer`, but every `Consumer` reference is the same.

The only condition under which you'd have unique producers *and* consumers is when both types are set to `prototype` scope – when the `Consumer` is retrieved from the context, a new `Producer` is created for it (since the `Producer` scope is `prototype`), and this process is followed for every `Consumer,` again, *assuming* both types are set to scope `prototype`. Otherwise, we might have separate and unique `Consumer` instances that share a `Producer` (i.e., `Consumer` is set to `prototype` but `Producer` is a singleton), or we have a single `Consumer` instance, and thus only one `Producer` is created for it (when `Consumer` is set to `singleton`).

Our last assertion validates the uniqueness of the `Producer` instances. If they are the same instance – i.e., it's *not* a prototype – the assertion tests that the `execute()` methods generate a sequence. If they are singletons, they won't generate sequential values like this.

However, we still can't *run* anything, because we don't have any configurations. Here are four configurations – note how they're largely the same, only differing in setting the scopes for each type.

In every case, we use `constructor-arg` to inject a `Producer` into a `Consumer` constructor.

Listing 4-6. `chapter04/src/test/resources/t1-noproto.xml`

```xml
<?xml version="1.0" encoding="UTF-8"?>
<beans xmlns="http://www.springframework.org/schema/beans"
       xmlns:xsi="http://www.w3.org/2001/XMLSchema-instance"
       xsi:schemaLocation="http://www.springframework.org/schema/beans
       http://www.springframework.org/schema/beans/spring-beans.xsd">
  <bean id="producer" class="c04.Producer"/>
  <bean id="consumer" class="c04.Consumer">
    <constructor-arg name="producer" ref="producer"/>
  </bean>
  <bean id="producerBean" class="java.lang.Boolean">
    <constructor-arg name="s" value="false" />
  </bean>
</beans>
```

Listing 4-7. chapter04/src/test/resources/t1-protoprod.xml

```xml
<?xml version="1.0" encoding="UTF-8"?>
<beans xmlns="http://www.springframework.org/schema/beans"
       xmlns:xsi="http://www.w3.org/2001/XMLSchema-instance"
       xsi:schemaLocation="http://www.springframework.org/schema/beans
       http://www.springframework.org/schema/beans/spring-beans.xsd">
  <bean id="producer" class="c04.Producer"
        scope="prototype"/>
  <bean id="consumer" class="c04.Consumer">
    <constructor-arg name="producer" ref="producer"/>
  </bean>
  <bean id="producerBean" class="java.lang.Boolean">
    <constructor-arg name="s" value="true" />
  </bean>
</beans>
```

Listing 4-8. chapter04/src/test/resources/t1-protocons.xml

```xml
<?xml version="1.0" encoding="UTF-8"?>
<beans xmlns="http://www.springframework.org/schema/beans"
       xmlns:xsi="http://www.w3.org/2001/XMLSchema-instance"
       xsi:schemaLocation="http://www.springframework.org/schema/beans
       http://www.springframework.org/schema/beans/spring-beans.xsd">
  <bean id="producer" class="c04.Producer" />
  <bean id="consumer" class="c04.Consumer"
        scope="prototype">
    <constructor-arg name="producer" ref="producer"/>
  </bean>
  <bean id="consumerBean" class="java.lang.Boolean">
    <constructor-arg name="s" value="true" />
  </bean>
</beans>
```

Listing 4-9. chapter04/src/test/resources/t1-protoboth.xml

```xml
<?xml version="1.0" encoding="UTF-8"?>
```

```xml
<beans xmlns="http://www.springframework.org/schema/beans"
       xmlns:xsi="http://www.w3.org/2001/XMLSchema-instance"
       xsi:schemaLocation="http://www.springframework.org/schema/beans
       http://www.springframework.org/schema/beans/spring-beans.xsd">
  <bean id="producer" class="c04.Producer"
        scope="prototype"/>
  <bean id="consumer" class="c04.Consumer"
        scope="prototype">
    <constructor-arg name="producer" ref="producer"/>
  </bean>
  <bean id="producerBean" class="java.lang.Boolean">
    <constructor-arg name="s" value="true"/>
  </bean>
  <bean id="consumerBean" class="java.lang.Boolean">
    <constructor-arg name="s" value="true"/>
  </bean>
</beans>
```

With these configurations, we have examples of every combination of scopes for our two classes:

1.   Everything is a singleton (and only two instances are created, period, and they're reused).

2.   Producer is a singleton and Consumer is a prototype; we create two Consumer references, but they have the same Producer.

3.   Consumer is a singleton and Producer is a prototype; we only create one Consumer (which gets a unique Producer), but requesting Producer references explicitly get new Producer references.

4.   Both Producer and Consumer are prototypes, and thus each Consumer gets a unique Producer reference.

Our logs even display this, although since they use reference ids, they'll look different for every execution. For one run of the test, for example, we see the following output, truncated to save (a lot of) space:

```
INFO c04.Producer - constructed as 93cf163
```

```
INFO c04.Consumer - constructed with producer 93cf163
INFO c04.Producer - constructed as 5c10f1c3
INFO c04.Producer - constructed as 7ac2e39b
INFO c04.Producer - constructed as 78365cfa
INFO c04.Consumer - constructed with producer 78365cfa
INFO c04.Producer - constructed as 3f6db3fb
INFO c04.Consumer - constructed with producer 3f6db3fb
INFO c04.Producer - constructed as 1506f20f
INFO c04.Consumer - constructed with producer 1506f20f
INFO c04.Consumer - constructed with producer 1506f20f
INFO c04.Producer - constructed as 19553973
INFO c04.Consumer - constructed with producer 19553973
INFO c04.Producer - constructed as 4c4748bf
INFO c04.Producer - constructed as 7ce97ee5
```

Note   If you're wondering, that output is created by piping the output of the test run into `cut -d ' ' -f 4-99 | grep c04 | grep -v spring`. The actual output is much longer and quite a bit more verbose. It's more informative, too, over the long run, but the extra information doesn't serve our purposes here.

Annotations

We can set scope with annotations as well, of course. The annotation itself is `org.springframework.context.annotation.Scope`, and it would look something like this:

Listing 4-10. chapter04/src/test/java/c04/AnnotatedProducer.java

```
package c04;

import org.slf4j.Logger;
import org.slf4j.LoggerFactory;
import org.springframework.context.annotation.Scope;
import org.springframework.stereotype.Component;
```

```
@Component
@Scope("singleton")
public class AnnotatedProducer {
    Logger logger = LoggerFactory.getLogger(this.getClass());
    int executions = 0;

  AnnotatedProducer() {
    logger.info("constructed");
  }

  int execute() {
    return ++executions;
  }
}
```

This class, loaded by a context, would be an exact duplicate of the producer references from our XML configurations, where the Producer is set to prototype scope. The *only* difference is in the use of annotations.

Note   We're not using AnnotatedProducer in any tests for this chapter, because there's no need – again, it's functionally identical to the XML configuration – and writing a test that can use the XML configuration *and* the annotations is more work than it's worth for our purposes. It would be long and complicated and need more explanation than anyone would really want.

Summary

In this chapter, we saw how two of the primary scope types work in Spring and how they affect object construction (and when).

CHAPTER 5

Using Resource Files

So far, we've put all of our data in *configurations* – whether as annotated source files or in XML configurations. In this chapter, we're going to look at some Spring features to help us use data from external files.

These external resources not only help us load the data we're using,[1] but they're also useful in separating out configuration, such as when you want to store secure data in external locations that shouldn't be part of your source code or in internationalization for people who may not speak the same language you do.

Injecting a Resource

The first thing we're going to do is create a configuration that provides a `org.springframework.core.io.Resource` – with the resource being something that holds the contents of a text file.

Let's start off by creating a `chapter05` project. The `build.gradle` is very straightforward; it's actually a *literal* copy of the `build.gradle` from Chapter 4.

Listing 5-1. `chapter05/build.gradle`

```
dependencies {
    implementation  \
      "org.springframework:spring-core:$springFrameworkVersion"
    implementation  \
      "org.springframework:spring-context:$springFrameworkVersion"
    implementation  \
      "org.springframework:spring-test:$springFrameworkVersion"
}
```

---

[1] Consider Listing 2-6, from Chapter 2, which had a long list of `new Document()` calls to populate a list of documents. We should – and can – load that from external resources.

© Felipe Gutierrez, Joseph B. Ottinger 2022
F. Gutierrez and J. B. Ottinger, *Introducing Spring Framework 6*, https://doi.org/10.1007/978-1-4842-8637-1_5

Don't forget to add `include 'chapter05'` to the top-level `settings.gradle`.

Let's keep it simple and create a text file that says `Hello, world` – this is boring and predictable, but we'll be validating the contents of the file in a test, so we *want* boring and predictable.

Listing 5-2. `chapter05/src/test/resources/hello.txt`

```
Hello, world
```

Note   Be careful about locations of the resources. Here, we've put `hello.txt` in our `src/test/resources` directory; what happens if we put it in `src/main/resources` as well, with different content? Resources are loaded through Java's classloaders, so whichever version happens to be available first in the classpath is the one that will get loaded. Normally, test resources get added to the beginning of the classpath on test runs, so the test version will be used... for tests.

Now for the fun part, let's create a test that asserts that the contents of `hello.txt` match `Hello, world` as we expect. We'll have two classes in one file, a configuration and a test, and the configuration is going to walk us through a few interesting things to note.

Listing 5-3. `chapter05/src/test/java/c05/ResourceInjectionTest.java`

```java
package c05;

import org.springframework.beans.factory.annotation.Autowired;
import org.springframework.context.annotation.Bean;
import org.springframework.context.annotation.Configuration;
import org.springframework.core.io.DefaultResourceLoader;
import org.springframework.core.io.Resource;
import org.springframework.test.context.ContextConfiguration;
import org.springframework.test.context.testng.
AbstractTestNGSpringContextTests;
import org.testng.annotations.Test;

import java.io.IOException;
import java.nio.charset.StandardCharsets;
import java.util.Scanner;
import static org.testng.Assert.assertEquals;
```

```
@Configuration
class ResourceInjectionConfig {
  @Bean
  public Resource getHelloWorldResource() {
    return new DefaultResourceLoader()
      .getResource("classpath:hello.txt");
  }

  @Bean
  String getContent(Resource resource) throws IOException {
    try(var scanner = new Scanner(
      resource.getInputStream(),
      StandardCharsets.UTF_8)
    ) {
      scanner.useDelimiter("\\A");
      return scanner.hasNext()?scanner.next().trim():"";
    }
  }
}

@ContextConfiguration(classes = {ResourceInjectionConfig.class})
public class ResourceInjectionTest
  extends AbstractTestNGSpringContextTests {
  @Autowired
  String helloWorld;

  @Test
  void testHelloWorld() {
    assertEquals(helloWorld, "Hello, world");
  }
}
```

The test itself is pretty straightforward: declare a configuration class
(ResourceInjectionConfig) and inject a String. The String is named helloWorld – but
the autowiring uses *type matching,* so it looks for beans that match the type of the value.
The only bean we have declared is returned from getContent(), so that's the method
that gets called to populate the value.

Our actual test itself merely validates the value of the autowired String. But how do we *get* the value in the first place?

Our configuration class looks more complicated (even with only two methods) that it might *need* to be. At the same time, though, we build it like this because this configuration demonstrates building a working configuration through composition, by breaking down what we need into small, simple pieces.

We have, after all, two processes in loading the resource:

1. The Resource retrieval itself, or "how do we get the resource"

2. The conversion of a Resource into a String, which happens when the value is retrieved for the first time, when the value is injected via @Autowired

Each of these is testable in and of itself.

The getContent() method is not particularly admirable; it uses a bit of a brute force, slow method of converting an InputStream to a String. Why, then, didn't we use a library like Guava (https://guava.dev) to do the work for us?

As usual, there are a few reasons:

1. I didn't want to add Guava solely for this one feature. Guava's an incredibly useful library, but adding a dependency for this one method felt very heavy.

2. Spring's scopes (see Chapter 4!) help us, by caching the value of getContent() for future invocations. The default scope is singleton; if we reuse the value 400 times, Spring will simply return the value it's already computed, rather than creating 400 instances of Scanner. We could show this in code, but Chapter 4 demonstrated scopes, and doing so in this chapter would add a lot of repetitive listings and it's just not worth it.

Loading Injected Values from Property Files

Spring can also inject values from property files into bean values.

While "My Documents" is a suitable name for our sample app – and we're going to stick with it – it would be nice if we were able to change it without having to recompile our application.

Let's load it from a property file, a feature that will serve us well in our Spring journey.

We can do this trivially through the use of two annotations: `@PropertySource` and `@Value`

`@PropertySource`, applied to the configuration class, basically create a bean itself that serves as a resource for use by the `@Value` annotation. It has a few properties, but only two are typically relevant: one is the `value` – the default property – which is a reference to the source of the properties. The other is `ignoreResourceNotFound`, a boolean value, which will silently ignore those cases where the resource could not be loaded. (The default for `ignoreResourceNotFound` is `false`.)

The resource name is a flexible name. Used in the most simple way possible, it's a reference to a resource in the classpath for Java. However, it's a URL, so you can use a *scheme* and a resource name to load resources.

A scheme is normally a reference to the type of resource loader should be used. If you have used the World Wide Web, you're probably familiar with schemes like `https` and `http`, `ftp`, or even `file`; browsers know how to handle resources that use these schemes as loaders. Spring's resource loader infers a custom scheme of `classpath` – which can also be used explicitly – to load resources from, well, the classpath.

Note   There's also a `classpath*` variant, which is a way of loading a wildcard for resources. It's particularly useful when you're trying to load a number of resources all at once, but we won't be using it in this chapter.

The other annotation that works for us here is `@Value`. It only has one property, a string that represents a lookup. This uses the "Spring Expression Language," also known as "SpEL," to parse expressions to derive values.

SpEL is *incredibly* powerful. It can not only look up values inside of objects (to arbitrary depths), but it can call methods on those objects, too, so theoretically you could use SpEL to invoke methods to communicate with a database, for example.

We're not going to go into massive depth of SpEL yet – we're going to use simple object lookups – but if you're interested, you can find the SpEL definition in Spring's documentation under "Spring Expression Language (SpEL)."[2]

---

[2] The "Spring Expression Language (SpEL)" documentation can be found at `https://docs.` `spring.io/spring-framework/docs/6.0.x/reference/html/core.html#expressions`.

Let's see these in action. We'll have two files: one is a resource file, menu.properties, and the other is a test class and a configuration. First, menu.properties is a very simple file indeed:

Listing 5-4. chapter05/src/test/resources/menu.properties

```
app.title=My Documents
```

Now, let's take a look at PropertyTest.java, which has a configuration class as well:

Listing 5-5. chapter05/src/test/java/c05/PropertyTest.java

```java
package c05;

import org.springframework.beans.factory.annotation.Autowired;
import org.springframework.beans.factory.annotation.Value;
import org.springframework.context.annotation.Bean;
import org.springframework.context.annotation.Configuration;
import org.springframework.context.annotation.PropertySource;
import org.springframework.test.context.ContextConfiguration;
import
org.springframework.test.context.testng.AbstractTestNGSpringContextTests;
import org.testng.annotations.Test;

import static org.testng.Assert.assertEquals;

@Configuration
@PropertySource("classpath:/menu.properties")
class PropertyConfiguration {
  @Value("${app.title}")
  String title;

  @Bean
  String getTitle() {
    return title;
  }
}

@ContextConfiguration(classes = {PropertyConfiguration.class})
public class PropertyTest
```

```
extends AbstractTestNGSpringContextTests {
  @Autowired
  String title;

  @Test
  void testTitle() {
    assertEquals(title, "My Documents");
  }
}
```

This test is not especially complicated. The PropertyConfiguration uses a @PropertySource to load menu.properties; it has one attribute, a String, called title, which is populated via @Value. The value attribute itself is app.title, which happens to match the one property we have in menu.properties, and the test validates that it matches what we expect.

The format of the @Value is quite simple: "${app.title}," which is a straightforward lookup in the property resource we specified in the PropertySource annotation.

Note   If you use @PropertySource() with ignoreResourceNotFound=true, then the @Value will not interpolate the resource – you'll get something like ${app.title} as the value instead of the value of the property. If ignoreResourceNotFound is left out, or is explicitly set to false, then the configuration will fail to load, with a FileNotFoundException.

Internationalization

Note   I desperately wanted to call this section Internationalization (or, perhaps, Internationalisation or ¡Internacionalización!). Thankfully, I have some measure of restraint even if my editor might not think so. Plus, the section title ended up being too long.

In "Injecting a Resource" – the previous section – we showed the mechanism of getting an InputStream from a Resource and converting the InputStream to a String. That's interesting, but not especially useful in and of itself. However, it *can* be useful – and necessary – in a world where more than one language is used.

Let's go a little further and show how one might use Java's internationalization to display an application's title based on locale.

In Listing 5-5, we saw how we could load menu.properties, but we can use similar mechanisms to look up resources based on locale and go even further.

Spring has the concept of a MessageSource, which provides us the ability to not only look up resources based on locale, but we can apply message formatting to the content, as well. It does so using the same rules as Java's java.text.MessageFormat class.

First, let's see two property files. The first is a "default locale" and is based on an English locale, and the other is based on Dutch.[3]

Listing 5-6. chapter05/src/test/resources/i18nmenu.properties

```
app.title=My Documents
app.greeting=Hello, {0}
app.copyright=(c) 2022 by Apress Media
```

Listing 5-7. chapter05/src/test/resources/i18nmenu_nl.properties

```
app.title=Mijn Documenten
app.greeting=Hallo, {0}
```

As we see, we have three properties – app.title and app.greeting and app.copyright – with app.copyright not being localized at all.

The app.greeting text uses a simple argument replacement structure, as per java.text.MessageFormat, and thus it will replace the {0} with the first argument in an array passed to the MessageSource.getMessage() method.

If we look up app.copyright in the MessageSource, it will fall back to the default messages, so we expect any lookup for app.copyright to return the English text.

Let's show this in action. We'll use three DataProvider methods so we can check each of the message types, and we'll pass in different locales so we can exercise all of the functionality.

---

[3] I do not speak or write Dutch; I used a translation service and hoped the messages were simple enough to be valid. If the Dutch here is not representative, I'll fix it as soon as I am able.

Listing 5-8. chapter05/src/test/java/c05/I18NTest.java

package c05;

import org.springframework.beans.factory.annotation.Autowired;
import org.springframework.context.MessageSource;
import org.springframework.context.annotation.Bean;
import org.springframework.context.annotation.Configuration;
import org.springframework.context.support.ResourceBundleMessageSource;
import org.springframework.test.context.ContextConfiguration;
import
org.springframework.test.context.testng.AbstractTestNGSpringContextTests;
import org.testng.annotations.DataProvider;
import org.testng.annotations.Test;

import java.util.Locale;

import static org.testng.Assert.assertEquals;

@Configuration
class I18NConfiguration {
  @Bean("messages")
  MessageSource getMessageSource() {
    var messageSource = **new** ResourceBundleMessageSource();
    messageSource.setBasename("i18nmenu");
    messageSource.setDefaultEncoding("UTF-8");
    return messageSource;
  }
}

@ContextConfiguration(classes = {I18NConfiguration.class})
public class I18NTest
  extends AbstractTestNGSpringContextTests {
  @Autowired
  MessageSource messages;

  @DataProvider
  Object[][] getTitleTranslations() {
    return new Object[][]{

```java
      {"en", "My Documents"},
      {"nl", "Mijn Documenten"}
    };
  }

  @DataProvider
  Object[][] getCopyrightTranslations() {
    return new Object[][]{
      {"en"},
      {"nl"},
    };
  }

  @DataProvider
  Object[][] getHelloTranslations() {
    return new Object[][]{
      {"en", "Hello, Joseph", "Joseph"},
      {"nl", "Hallo, Mattijs", "Mattijs"}
    };
  }

  @Test(dataProvider = "getTitleTranslations")
  void testTitle(String encoding, String translation) {
    assertEquals(
      messages.getMessage("app.title", null, new Locale(encoding)),
      translation);
  }

  @Test(dataProvider = "getHelloTranslations")
  void testGreeting(String encoding, String translation, String name) {
    assertEquals(
      messages.getMessage(
        "app.greeting",
        new Object[]{name},
        new Locale(encoding)
      ),
```

```
      translation);
  }

  @Test(dataProvider = "getCopyrightTranslations")
  void testCopyright(String encoding) {
    assertEquals(
      messages.getMessage("app.copyright", null, new Locale(encoding)),
      "(c) 2022 by Apress Media"
    );
  }
}
```

Enterprising multilingual readers are invited to add extra translations to explore the possibilities.

Summary

In this chapter, we've explored the use of resource files to set values in our configurations. We've also seen how we can use MessageSource to internationalize our output somewhat.

PART II

The Spring Framework

CHAPTER 6

Adding Simple Persistence to Your Spring Application

In this chapter, we're going to look at the beginnings of data storage outside of our application code. So far, we've been storing all of our data in an `Enum` and in our static search engines (with minor exceptions to show loading from configurations), but in the real world, relational databases are the standard data repositories. We're going to look at data access objects – DAOs – and how to set up database connections and move data out of our database.[1]

Persistence As a Concept

The idiomatic Java approach to using a database is fairly simple. To interact with a database, you:

1. Acquire a database connection.

2. Start a transaction.

3. Create a SQL statement.

4. Execute the SQL statement.

5. Interpret the results.

---

[1] We're not going to demonstrate *writing into* the database yet. That's going to show up in a later chapter. We promise. We're introducing concepts in small bites, and we're advancing rapidly into more functionality.

© Felipe Gutierrez, Joseph B. Ottinger 2022
F. Gutierrez and J. B. Ottinger, *Introducing Spring Framework 6*, https://doi.org/10.1007/978-1-4842-8637-1_6

6. Close the transaction.

7. Close the database connection.

Of course, errors can occur at multiple points in this process, and error handling would break the order.

Spring respects this model, but it also hides a lot of the infrastructure from your actual code. This is a massive benefit, in general, because it means that your code can focus on what it is actually doing, rather than on the typical plumbing associated with interacting with a database.

To interact with a relational database in Spring, we are going to set up a database connection in our configurations and configure a *template* class that handles actually using the connection. The template class gives us simple methods to issue SQL – `queryForObject`, `update`, and the like – and manages the underlying connection for us, as well as (potentially) handling the mapping of our results into Java objects.

With all that said, however, you should be aware that there are other ways to interact with databases; this is one among many. It's probably the simplest, and our next chapter will go into something far more powerful (and portable).

Revisiting Our Simple Data Model

For the purposes of this chapter, we are going to simplify our document data. So far, we have had two classes: `Document` and `DocumentType`, with `DocumentType` being a Java enum type (a predetermined list of possibilities). We're going to focus only on `Document` for this chapter and leave `DocumentType` as an exercise for the next chapter.

Our `Document` is going to look slightly different than what we've seen, because we're not including a `DocumentType` and we're adding an `id` field as an artificial identifier for the documents, much like a serial number.

It's a fairly long class, mostly because of boilerplate code for the mutators and accessors; for the sake of simplicity (and because our examples here don't need them), we're not including `equals()` and `hashCode()` methods. We're also going to include the `DocumentType` class, which is also part of our model. These classes are very similar to prior versions of the entities we've seen in prior chapters, with the main difference being the addition of an artificial identifier for the `Document` class.

Note   We could have used the new `record` type in Java for Document. Given that we never modify our data, it wouldn't have been a stretch, and the mechanism we are going to demonstrate for working with our data would work quite well with records. However, some of our later chapters will revisit persistence with mutable types, and records are less suitable there; we're going to stick with the simple approach for now.

Listing 6-1. chapter06/src/main/java/c06/Document.java

```java
package c06;

public class Document {
  private Integer id;
  private String name;
  private String location;
  private DocumentType type;

  public Document(int id, String name, DocumentType type, String
  location) {
    this.id=id;
    this.name=name;
    this.type=type;
    this.location=location;
  }
  public Document() {
  }

  public Integer getId() {
    return id;
  }

  public void setId(Integer id) {
    this.id = id;
  }

  public String getName() {
    return name;
  }
}
```

```java
  public void setName(String name) {
    this.name = name;
  }

  public String getLocation() {
    return location;
  }

  public void setLocation(String location) {
    this.location = location;
  }

  public DocumentType getType() {
    return type;
  }

  public void setType(DocumentType type) {
    this.type = type;
  }

  public String toString() {
    return String.format(
      "%s[name=%s,type=%s,location=%s]",
      this.getClass().getName(),
      name,
      type,
      location
    );
  }

  // we're not including equals() or hashcode() because this is
  // purely demo code and our tests don't use them.
}
```

Listing 6-2. chapter06/src/main/java/c06/DocumentType.java

```java
package c06;

public enum DocumentType {
  PDF("PDF", "Portable Document Format", ".pdf"),
  DOCX("DOCX", "Word Document", ".docx"),
```

```
  URL("URL", "Universal Resource Locator", ""),
  DOC("DOC", "Word Document", ".doc"),
  NOTE("NOTE", "Ancillary note", "");

  public final String name;
  public final String desc;
  public final String extension;

  DocumentType(String name, String desc, String extension) {
    this.name=name;
    this.desc=desc;
    this.extension=extension;
  }
}
```

> **Note**   Our enum here uses public attributes for the specific values to save space and for no other reason. Otherwise, we have another 12 lines of code, at the very least, that contribute nothing to our understanding of the data model. Given that the values are `final`, we are losing no functionality to gain brevity.

We are now ready to look at our actual database.

Choosing a Database

We have a lot of options for relational databases;[2] we're limited **only** by whether a JDBC driver exists for them or not, and there are few (if any) relational databases for which JDBC drivers are not available.

Options include databases like Oracle DB, MySQL, SQL Server, PostgreSQL, DB2, and SQLite – and this is hardly an exhaustive list. In fact, we're going to use a database that's *not* on this list, called H2.

---

[2] We keep mentioning *relational* databases because this chapter is focused on databases that use SQL. They're the most common type of database in the field, but there are other non-SQL databases; we're going to mention some of them in the next chapter, but we're still going to focus on relationals because when you say "database," relational databases are what people usually think you're talking about.

H2 (`www.h2database.com/`) is an open source database engine that was designed to be embedded in a JVM (although it can run as a separate server process, much like most other relational databases). There's no issue in having preferences for other databases, but note that the SQL in this chapter caters *slightly* to H2.

As we'll see, Spring itself encourages use of H2, with support for a database for testing purposes. We'll see that in use in Listing 6-4.

Setting Up a JDBC Connection

Java uses the concept of a `DriverManager` to control database connections. Generally speaking, one registers a JDBC driver (by putting it in the JVM classpath, as Java has a discovery mechanism for JDBC drivers) and requests a database connection by specifying a JDBC URL to a database along with a username and password.

Note   You can learn about the basics of JDBC from the Java Tutorial. See `https://docs.oracle.com/javase/tutorial/jdbc/basics/index.html` for more; it's relevant for us here but is out of scope for this book.

Spring has a class available for use in Spring contexts, the `org.springframework.jdbc.datasource.DriverManagerDataSource`. We're going to configure it using property placeholders, so we can easily change the values the connection uses, through the use of a `<context:property-placeholder/>` tag in our XML configuration.

Note   We've used a lot of Java configuration for Spring so far. Here, we're using XML. This is just a style choice made for this chapter; there's nothing preventing us from doing the same in Java, and this gives us a chance to explore more of the XML capabilities.

Before we go too much further, let's build our `build.gradle` file, which has a two new dependencies for this book: the H2 database and spring-jdbc, which gives us the ability to construct our database on context startup.[3]

---

[3] We're going to describe database initialization very soon in this chapter.

Listing 6-3. `chapter06/build.gradle`

```
dependencies {
    implementation  \
      "org.springframework:spring-core:$springFrameworkVersion"
    implementation  \
      "org.springframework:spring-context:$springFrameworkVersion"
    implementation  \
      "org.springframework:spring-test:$springFrameworkVersion"
    implementation  \
      "org.springframework:spring-jdbc:$springFrameworkVersion"
    implementation  \
      "com.h2database:h2:2.1.214"
}
```

Now we can look at our Spring configuration. It's got references to two classes we don't have source for yet, along with a reference to a JDBCTemplate instance, which we're *also* going to explain in an upcoming section in this chapter.[4]

Now that we have our build script, let's take a look at the configuration for this chapter. We want to zero in on the dataSource bean and the things that go into configuring it, first.

Note   The configuration file is in our test structure, as it's generally customized for our test code.

Listing 6-4. `chapter06/src/test/resources/explicit.xml`

```xml
<?xml version="1.0" encoding="UTF-8"?>
<beans xmlns="http://www.springframework.org/schema/beans"
       xmlns:xsi="http://www.w3.org/2001/XMLSchema-instance"
       xmlns:context="http://www.springframework.org/schema/context"
```

---

[4] There's an awful lot of "we're going to explain this later" in programming, unfortunately. It's largely unavoidable, because a lot of programming is about tying concepts together, and you sometimes have to describe the tying-together part before you can describe the concepts' relevance and application, especially when you're writing about technologies like Spring, which are *all about* the tying-together bits.

```
      xmlns:jdbc="http://www.springframework.org/schema/jdbc"
      xsi:schemaLocation="http://www.springframework.org/schema/beans
      http://www.springframework.org/schema/beans/spring-beans.xsd
      http://www.springframework.org/schema/context
      http://www.springframework.org/schema/context/spring-context.xsd
      http://www.springframework.org/schema/jdbc
      http://www.springframework.org/schema/jdbc/spring-jdbc.xsd">
  <context:property-placeholder location="jdbc.properties"/>

  <bean id="c6DataSource"
        class="org.springframework.jdbc.datasource.
        DriverManagerDataSource">
    <property name="driverClassName" value="${jdbc.driverClassName}"/>
    <property name="url" value="${jdbc.url}"/>
    <property name="username" value="${jdbc.username}"/>
    <property name="password" value="${jdbc.password}"/>
  </bean>

  <jdbc:embedded-database id="c6DataSource" type="H2">
    <jdbc:script location="classpath:/schema.sql"/>
    <jdbc:script location="classpath:/import.sql"/>
  </jdbc:embedded-database>

  <bean id="jdbcTemplate"
        class="org.springframework.jdbc.core.JdbcTemplate">
    <property name="dataSource" ref="c6DataSource"/>
  </bean>

  <bean id="engine" class="c06.SearchEngineService">
    <property name="dao" ref="documentDAO" />
  </bean>

  <bean id="documentDAO" class="c06.DocumentJDBCDAO">
    <property name="template" ref="jdbcTemplate" />
  </bean>
</beans>
```

The only interesting thing about the configuration so far is the use of `jdbc.properties`, which is a simple and straightforward property file. It's in our `main` directory, as we're going to reuse it in a later chapter. For this chapter, it looks like this:

Listing 6-5. `chapter06/src/main/resources/jdbc.properties`

```
jdbc.driverClassName=org.h2.Driver
jdbc.url=jdbc:h2:mem:chapter6
jdbc.username=sa
jdbc.password=
```

The next thing we're going to look at is the `<jdbc:embedded-database/>` tag. This is a convenience directive that accepts a `DataSource` and can run scripts on initialization. We also specify the *type* of the database as H2, as the default is HSQLDB.[5]

We see in our configuration that we're running `schema.sql` and `data.sql` from our classpath; these set up our schema and populate our schema with data, respectively. We could have done them in the same file, but from an organizational standpoint, it's better to separate the initializations.

Note   Spring Data uses the same kind of initialization, where you can have a schema and a dataset available – under these names, even. It's just implicit in Spring Data and explicit given how we're building our data access in *this* chapter.

First, here's our schema for the `Document` type, which is very simple:

Listing 6-6. `chapter06/src/main/resources/schema.sql`

```
CREATE TABLE document (
    id identity primary key,
    name varchar(255) not null,
    type varchar(16) not null,
    location varchar(255) not null
);
```

---

[5] HSQLDB and H2 are both embeddable databases descended from Thomas Mueller's original HSQL database. Both are open source; they're functionally very near equivalents; H2 is Thomas Mueller's own fork of HSQL.

Note   Porting to a different database would mostly involve changing the `id` field to match an autogenerated integer field as a primary key. Everything else would generally be compatible.

Here's our "initial dataset" for the documents, matching the data we've used for our SearchEngine through the rest of the book:

Listing 6-7. `chapter06/src/main/resources/import.sql`

```
insert into document (id, name, type, location)
values (
        1,
        'Book Template',
        'PDF',
        '/Docs/Template.pdf'
       );
insert into document (id, name, type, location)
values (
          2,
          'Apress Home Page',
          'URL',
          'https://apress.com'
       );
insert into document (id, name, type, location)
values (
          3,
          'Chapter Template',
          'DOC',
          '/Docs/Chapter Sample.doc'
       );
insert into document (id, name, type, location)
values (
          4,
          'chapter 1',
          'DOCX',
```

```
    '/Book/Chapter 01.docx'
);
```

Now that we have our database built, we can look at the JDBCTemplate.

The JDBCTemplate

The Spring documentation describes JDBCTemplate as the "central class in the JDBC core package." It provides a number of methods to ease access to operations enabled by a Connection, such as executing SQL via PreparedStatement. It manages access to the database connection, provides implicit exception translation for easier declaration and handling of exceptions,[6] and also provides easy access to mapping database information into Java classes, although often not at the level of mappings that an object-relational mapper like Hibernate can provide.

Note   Spring has *multiple* easy ways to leverage Hibernate and other object-relational mappers, too. The most convenient is through Spring Data, which we'll look at in a later chapter.

If you're not going to use Spring Data – and you should, honestly, as it provides an incredible level of control and freedom to your code – you'll want to spend some time mastering JDBCTemplate. Luckily, it's a simple class – albeit with a huge list of methods – and mastery is fairly trivial.

Let's look at more source code and make our document manager database-aware at last.

---

[6] JDBCTemplate converts common SQLException instances to specific types of exceptions that reflect the actual errors, rather than having generic exceptions. For example, instead of a SQLException with an error code of 42101, you would get a BadSqlGrammarException – with the code being one of H2's error codes for bad SQL grammar.

Our Service Interfaces and the SearchEngine Implementation

It's time for us to start working with our entity model from Listings 6-1 and 6-2. Let's take a look at the SearchEngine interface, itself a near-literal copy from prior chapters. It's worth noting that the return type from the methods extends List and not Set; Set implies a unique set of instances (which fits what we want), but you can't access the objects in order (they *have* an order, but we can't access them trivially). List provides explicit order but has no guarantee of uniqueness. For simplicity, we're using List.

Listing 6-8. chapter06/src/main/java/c06/SearchEngine.java

```java
package c06;

import java.util.List;

public interface SearchEngine {
  List<Document> findByType(DocumentType documentType);

  List<Document> listAll();
}
```

And finally, a new interface, the DocumentDAO, which defines those operations that a "Document data-access object" would need to provide. Due to the simplicity of what we're demonstrating, it has direct mappings to the SearchEngine – we could have skipped this interface altogether, but in a real application, a DAO will have simpler service methods than the SearchEngine would and would map less cleanly.

Listing 6-9. chapter06/src/main/java/c06/DocumentDAO.java

```java
package c06;

import java.util.List;

public interface DocumentDAO {
  List<Document> findByType(DocumentType documentType);

  List<Document> listAll();
}
```

It's worth noting that this isn't *really* what most people would consider a full-featured data access object: it's read-only, and rather sparse. You will also encounter classes named "DAO" rather rarely in the Spring ecosystem, except in really old code; you're far more likely to see classes that are named "repositories" instead, as there's a base type in Spring Data called Repository that does indeed implement a full set of reads and writes for entities. We'll be going over Spring Data in the next chapters and explore reading and writing further.

Now that we have our interfaces defined, we get to see some implementations, at last. First, let's look at the SearchEngineService, an implementation of SearchEngine that delegates to an instance of DocumentDAO.

Listing 6-10. chapter06/src/main/java/c06/SearchEngineService.java

```java
package c06;

import java.util.List;

public class SearchEngineService implements SearchEngine {
  private DocumentDAO dao;

  public void setDao(DocumentDAO dao) {
    this.dao = dao;
  }

  public DocumentDAO getDao() {
    return dao;
  }

  @Override
  public List<Document> findByType(DocumentType documentType) {
    return getDao().findByType(documentType);
  }

  @Override
  public List<Document> listAll() {
    return getDao().listAll();
  }
}
```

The main thing to look for in SearchEngineService is the use of an attribute for the DocumentDAO. Since the methods in the SearchEngine and the DocumentDAO align so cleanly, we simply delegate to the DocumentDAO.

At last, we get to something actually interesting to see: the DocumentJDBCDAO, so named because it's a Document DAO that focuses on JDBC as the underlying storage mechanism.

Listing 6-11. chapter06/src/main/java/c06/DocumentJDBCDAO.java

```java
package c06;

import org.springframework.jdbc.core.JdbcTemplate;

import java.util.List;

public class DocumentJDBCDAO implements DocumentDAO {
  private JdbcTemplate template;
  public void setTemplate(JdbcTemplate template) {
    this.template = template;
  }

  private JdbcTemplate getTemplate() {
    return template;
  }

  @Override
  public List<Document> listAll() {
    return getTemplate()
      .query(
        "select * from document",
        new DocumentMapper()
      );
  }

  @Override
  public List<Document> findByType(DocumentType documentType) {
    return getTemplate()
      .query("select * from document d where d.type=?",
```

```
    ps -> ps.setString(1, documentType.name()),
    new DocumentMapper()
  );

 }

}
```

There are two main things to notice in Document JDBCDAO. The first is quite simple: the `template` attribute, which is how we provide access to a database via the JDBCTemplate. The other thing is, of course, the use of the `template` itself.

We use it in two ways. One is via simple SQL, in the `listAll` method. We are issuing a simple and straightforward query, in SQL, and we provide a DocumentMapper instance to the method so it can convert each row in the result to a Document.

Here's what DocumentMapper looks like:

Listing 6-12. chapter06/src/main/java/c06/DocumentMapper.java

```
package c06;

import org.springframework.jdbc.core.RowMapper;

import java.sql.ResultSet;
import java.sql.SQLException;

class DocumentMapper implements RowMapper<Document> {
  @Override
  public Document mapRow(ResultSet rs, int rowNum) throws SQLException {
    Document document=new Document();
    document.setId(rs.getInt("id"));
    document.setLocation(rs.getString("location"));
    document.setType(DocumentType.valueOf(rs.getString("type")));
    document.setName(rs.getString("name"));
    return document;
  }
}
```

This has a single method (`mapRow`) and could have been a lambda, but that's a poor choice for this use case, as we're likely to want to map rows in multiple places. A `DocumentMapper` can be used to map a single row from SQL for a specific query, for example, but can also be used to map large numbers of rows; thus, we're better off creating a class for it; it's a functional interface, so we **can** describe a lambda for the operation, but lambdas have performance and garbage collection implications that we'd like to avoid.[7]

The last remaining method in `DocumentJDBCDAO` is interesting, because it uses a `PreparedStatementSetter` to control query parameters, as a lambda. It receives a `PreparedStatement` (from `JDBCTemplate`) and can call the various `set` methods as desired, such that we can issue a query safe from SQL injection while still leveraging all of the convenience features that `JDBCTemplate` gives.

There are a *lot* of features `JDBCTemplate` exposes. However, we're not going to dig into them, because in general you're better off using an object-relational mapper or, even better, Spring Data.

Tying It All Together

So we've seen *11* source files to build a search engine, but we've seen nothing actually using the structure.

Building a test, though, ends up being anticlimactic. This is probably a *good* thing – a test that wasn't anticlimactic would mean that we still had a lot of explanation to go through.

Our test is modeled after some of our earlier tests, much as some of our search engine implementation has been.

Listing 6-13. chapter06/src/test/java/c06/MyDocsTest.java

```
package c06;

import org.springframework.beans.factory.annotation.Autowired;
import org.springframework.test.context.ContextConfiguration;
```

---

[7] Lambdas are **not** problems for garbage collectors, as long as you reuse the same lambda reference. If we have the same body for a lambda, over and over again, we're actually creating independent anonymous classes, and those *do* have negative implications for garbage collection. It's simpler, for the purposes of this book, to just create the functional interface as a concrete class.

```java
import org.springframework.test.context.testng.AbstractTestNGSpring
ContextTests;
import org.testng.annotations.Test;

import static c06.DocumentType.PDF;
import static org.testng.Assert.assertEquals;
import static org.testng.Assert.assertNotNull;

@ContextConfiguration(locations={"classpath:/explicit.xml"})
public class MyDocsTest extends AbstractTestNGSpringContextTests {
  @Autowired
  SearchEngine engine;

  SearchEngine getEngine() {
    return engine;
  };

  @Test
  void testEngineNonNull() {
    assertNotNull(getEngine());
  }

  @Test
  void testFindByType() {
    var documents = getEngine().findByType(PDF);
    assertNotNull(documents);
    assertEquals(documents.size(), 1);
    assertEquals(PDF.name,
      documents.get(0).getType().name);
    assertEquals(PDF.desc,
      documents.get(0).getType().desc);
    assertEquals(PDF.extension,
      documents.get(0).getType().extension);
  }

  @Test
  void testListAll() {
    var documents = getEngine().listAll();
```

```
    assertNotNull(documents);
    assertEquals(documents.size(), 4);
  }

}
```

As you can see, it's really quite simple. The main difference between this and other tests is the configuration itself. After that, we have a test to make sure that the engine attribute is properly populated, and we have a few of our tests from previous chapters to verify that our results look like what we expect.

Summary

In this chapter, we've seen how to build a DataSource in Spring, and we've built a set of interfaces that provide a workable data access layer and implemented those interfaces.

In our next chapter, we're going to take a look at Spring Data, which makes most of *this* chapter unnecessary except as a springboard for concepts.

CHAPTER 7

Letting Spring Build Your Data Access Objects

In Chapter 6, we saw how we can build a data access object using JDBC, configured with Spring. In this chapter, we're going to take a look at Spring Data, which provides a bridge to other underlying persistence mechanisms – the Java Persistence API, in this case, using Hibernate as an underlying implementation.

Hibernate is an "object-relational mapper,"[1] meaning that it's a library that maps data between the object and relational models. (In regular human language, it takes Java objects and stores them in a relational database or loads relational data into an object model.)

It's important to know what object-relational mapping is; for most real Java applications, it's considered foundational knowledge in many cases – but for us, it's enough to know that it's in common use, and Spring Data provides a trivial way to leverage it.

Let's dive in.

The Project

Our build.gradle comes first. It calls back rather heavily to the Spring Boot build in Chapter 2, in that it has a plug-in for Boot itself, as well as the dependency manager; the dependencies it brings in include Spring Data JPA, Boot's test framework, TestNG, and – lastly – the H2 database.

---

[1] If "object-relational mapper" as a term feels familiar to you, it's because we mentioned it in passing in the last chapter or because you've paid attention to the Java ecosystem a touch in the last few years.

© Felipe Gutierrez, Joseph B. Ottinger 2022
F. Gutierrez and J. B. Ottinger, *Introducing Spring Framework 6*, https://doi.org/10.1007/978-1-4842-8637-1_7

Listing 7-1. `chapter07/build.gradle`

```
plugins {
    id 'org.springframework.boot' version '3.0.0-M3'
    id 'io.spring.dependency-management' version '1.0.11.RELEASE'
}

dependencies {
    implementation \
      "org.springframework.boot:spring-boot-starter-data-jpa"
    implementation \
      "org.springframework.boot:spring-boot-starter-test"
    testImplementation \
      "org.testng:testng:$testNgVersion"
    implementation  \
      "com.h2database:h2:2.1.214"
}
```

Next, let's take a look at the data model – the `DocumentType` and `Document` classes, which will be very (*very*) similar to the classes we saw in Chapter 6. The biggest difference is in `Document`, because we're adding JPA mapping annotations to the class; we have to define the entity and its primary key, at the very least. We could do so with XML configuration files for Hibernate or JPA, but the simplest and most common approach is to use annotations as we've done here. The only "interesting" aspect to the mapping is for the `type` field, which we're mapping as a `String` to match our data model from Chapter 6.

Listing 7-2. `chapter07/src/main/java/c07/Document.java`

```
package c07;

import jakarta.persistence.*;

@Entity
public class Document {
  @Id
  Integer id;
  @Column(nullable = false)
```

```
String name;
@Column(nullable = false)
String location;
@Column(nullable = false)
@Enumerated(EnumType.STRING)
DocumentType type;

public Integer getId() {
  return id;
}

public void setId(Integer id) {
  this.id = id;
}

public String getName() {
  return name;
}

public void setName(String name) {
  this.name = name;
}

public String getLocation() {
  return location;
}

public void setLocation(String location) {
  this.location = location;
}

public DocumentType getType() {
  return type;
}

public void setType(DocumentType type) {
  this.type = type;
}
}
```

Our DocumentType enum is effectively copy-pasted from Chapter 6,[2] with only the package declaration being different.

Listing 7-3. chapter07/src/main/java/c07/DocumentType.java

```
package c07;

public enum DocumentType {
  PDF("PDF", "Portable Document Format", ".pdf"),
  DOCX("DOCX", "Word Document", ".docx"),
  URL("URL", "Universal Resource Locator", ""),
  DOC("DOC", "Word Document", ".doc"),
  NOTE("NOTE", "Ancillary note", "");

  public final String name;
  public final String desc;
  public final String extension;

  DocumentType(String name, String desc, String extension) {
    this.name=name;
    this.desc=desc;
    this.extension=extension;
  }
}
```

Next, let's take a look at our SearchEngine structure. The SearchEngine itself is going to be what we've already seen: an interface with two methods.

Listing 7-4. chapter07/src/main/java/c07/SearchEngine.java

```
package c07;

import java.util.List;

public interface SearchEngine {
  List<Document> findByType(DocumentType documentType);

  List<Document> listAll();
}
```

---

[2] We're going to be copying things wholesale again in the next chapter, too.

We're also going to have a concrete implementation, very similar to the
DAOSearchEngine from Chapter 6, except as we're going to use a Spring Data
Repository, we're going to call it the RepositorySearchEngine. The purpose of this class
is to delegate to a DocumentRepository, which we'll see very soon.

Listing 7-5. chapter07/src/main/java/c07/RepositorySearchEngine.java

```java
package c07;

import org.springframework.beans.factory.annotation.Autowired;

import java.util.ArrayList;
import java.util.List;

public class RepositorySearchEngine implements SearchEngine {
  private final DocumentRepository dao;

  public RepositorySearchEngine(DocumentRepository repository) {
    this.dao = repository;
  }

  public DocumentRepository getDao() {
    return dao;
  }

  @Override
  public List<Document> findByType(DocumentType documentType) {
    return getDao().findByType(documentType);
  }

  @Override
  public List<Document> listAll() {
    var documents = new ArrayList<Document>();
    getDao().findAll().forEach(documents::add);
    return documents;
  }
}
```

Note that we don't have an annotation marking this as a @Service, we're going to define a configuration in Java that provides access to the bean, as opposed to relying on scanning. We *could* use scanning, but in practical reality you'll see a mix of approaches.

We'll want to have seed data, so we're going to reuse the import.sql from Chapter 6. Note that we don't need a schema.sql equivalent – we're going to let Spring Data create the schema, even though this is probably unwise in a production environment. (We will, however, have to direct Hibernate to accept multiline SQL statements, because otherwise they're too long to print cleanly.)

Note   Spring Data will use import.sql from the classpath any time it knows it needs to create the schema. As we're using an in-memory database, no schema will exist, and Spring Boot will run the import for us.

Listing 7-6. chapter07/src/main/resources/import.sql

```
insert into document (id, name, type, location)
values (
        1,
        'Book Template',
        'PDF',
        '/Docs/Template.pdf'
       );
insert into document (id, name, type, location)
values (
          2,
          'Apress Home Page',
          'URL',
          'https://apress.com'
       );
insert into document (id, name, type, location)
values (
          3,
          'Chapter Template',
          'DOC',
```

```
        '/Docs/Chapter Sample.doc'
    );
insert into document (id, name, type, location)
values (
        4,
        'chapter 1',
        'DOCX',
        '/Book/Chapter 01.docx'
    );
```

We can tell Hibernate to accept the multiline SQL through the use of `application.properties`:

Listing 7-7. `chapter07/src/main/resources/application.properties`

```
spring.jpa.properties.hibernate.hbm2ddl\
  .import_files_sql_extractor=org.hibernate\
  .tool.hbm2ddl.MultipleLinesSqlCommandExtractor
```

There are, of course, many other properties one can set for Hibernate in the configuration file.[3]

At long last, we're ready to look at the `Repository` itself.

Spring Data Repositories

Spring Data provides a `CrudRepository<Type, PrimaryKeyType>` interface, which has two type parameters: the type of the class being persisted (`Document` in this chapter) and the type of the primary key associated with the class being persisted (`Integer`, for `Document`).

The `CrudRepository<?,?>` interface provides access to a number of fairly standardizable operations one might want associated with a data access object:

---

[3] See `https://docs.spring.io/spring-boot/docs/current/reference/html/application-properties.html` for a *partial* list of properties. Ironically, the one we're using here isn't in this list.

save(T)	This saves the entity passed to it and returns an instance suitable for further operations.
saveAll(Iterable<T>)	This method takes an iterable collection of entities and returns a collection of entities suitable for further persistence operations, much as save() does for individual objects.
findById(ID)	This method looks up an entity using the parameter as a primary key. It returns an Optional<T> – if the primary key doesn't exist, the Optional will contain a null value.
existsById(ID)	This returns a boolean value indicating whether the primary key exists in the data store.
findAll()	This returns an Iterable<T> that contains all instances of the type in the data store.
findAllById(Iterable<ID>)	This returns an Iterable<T> for every instance in the database that has a matching identifier in the set of ids. If a given id does not exist in the database, it simply won't be included in the returned Iterable<T>.
count()	This returns the number of entities managed in the data store for this type.
deleteById(ID)	This deletes a matching record in the data store for this id.
delete(T)	This deletes a given entity, assuming it exists in the database.
deleteAllById(Iterable<ID>)	This deletes all matching id entries in the data store.
deleteAll(Iterable<T>)	This deletes all entries that have matches in the Iterable from the data store (i.e., "delete records that match the collection passed in").
deleteAll()	This clears the data store of all entities.

As you can see, this is quite flexible for most operations one would want with a data access object; there's another implementation, the PagingAndSortingRepository<?,?>, that adds the ability to iterate through a dataset with pagination.

There's a lot of magic provided by Spring with the Repository interfaces. Basically, to get everything the CrudRepository<?,?> provides, all we *have* to do is define a *single* interface that extends the CrudRepository<?,?>, adding the type information Spring needs.

We've had an awful lot of buildup for the actual `DocumentRepository`, but here it is, all of it:

Listing 7-8. `chapter07/src/main/java/c07/DocumentRepository.java`

```
package c07;

import org.springframework.data.repository.CrudRepository;
import org.springframework.stereotype.Repository;

import java.util.List;

@Repository
public interface DocumentRepository
  extends CrudRepository<Document, Integer> {
  List<Document> findByType(DocumentType type);
}
```

Note the `findByType` method. Spring will intercept this method and interpolate a valid query (based on the storage engine, which is JPA in this case), such that we don't even have to define a valid JPA query anywhere: we just say, "Oh, we'd like to do a search using the `type` field," and Spring will build it for us.

There's a full grammar for determining the query, which can include pagination, order, distinctions, and other elements; you can read about the full grammar at `https://docs.spring.io/spring-data/jpa/docs/current/reference/html/#repositories.query-methods.details`. There are ways to create shortcuts (and custom queries) for Repository instances, but they're out of scope for this chapter.

Let's show this structure in action. The main thing we need to do is tell our configuration to enable Spring Data JPA, by using the `@EnableJpaRepositories` annotation; everything else is fairly standard. Here's our `MyDocsConfiguration` class, which is part of our testing structure.

Listing 7-9. `chapter07/src/test/java/c07/MyDocsConfiguration.java`

```
package c07;

import org.springframework.beans.factory.annotation.Autowired;
import org.springframework.context.annotation.Bean;
import org.springframework.context.annotation.Configuration;
import org.springframework.data.jpa.repository.config.EnableJpaRepositories;
```

```
@Configuration
@EnableJpaRepositories
public class MyDocsConfiguration {
  @Bean
  SearchEngine getEngine(DocumentRepository repository) {
    return new RepositorySearchEngine(repository);
  }
}
```

After this, our actual test is child's play:

Listing 7-10. chapter07/src/test/java/c07/MyDocsTest.java

```
package c07;

import org.springframework.beans.factory.annotation.Autowired;
import org.springframework.boot.autoconfigure.EnableAutoConfiguration;
import org.springframework.boot.test.autoconfigure.orm.jpa.DataJpaTest;
import org.springframework.test.context.ContextConfiguration;
import org.springframework.test.context.testng.AbstractTestNGSpringContextTests;
import org.testng.annotations.Test;

import javax.sql.DataSource;

import static c07.DocumentType.PDF;
import static org.testng.Assert.assertEquals;
import static org.testng.Assert.assertNotNull;

@ContextConfiguration(classes = {MyDocsConfiguration.class})
@DataJpaTest
@EnableAutoConfiguration
public class
MyDocsTest extends AbstractTestNGSpringContextTests {
  @Autowired
  SearchEngine engine;

  @Autowired
  DataSource ds;
```

```java
SearchEngine getEngine() {
  return engine;
};

@Test
void testEngineNonNull() {
  assertNotNull(ds);
  assertNotNull(getEngine());
}

@Test
void testFindByType() {
  var documents = getEngine().findByType(PDF);
  assertNotNull(documents);
  assertEquals(documents.size(), 1);
  assertEquals(PDF.name,
    documents.get(0).getType().name);
  assertEquals(PDF.desc,
    documents.get(0).getType().desc);
  assertEquals(PDF.extension,
    documents.get(0).getType().extension);
}

@Test
void testListAll() {
  var documents = getEngine().listAll();
  assertNotNull(documents);
  assertEquals(documents.size(), 4);
}

}
```

The annotations we add to the test (@DataJpaTest and @EnableAutoConfiguration) establish the dependencies the Spring container needs to apply for the test, like creating the embedded database and a reference to it.

Summary

This is a lightning-speed tour of Spring Data, which provides an easy, common layer between our application code and a data store. This chapter used JPA (and thus the data store was a relational database), but adapters exist for a number of other persistence mechanisms, like JDBC (thus invalidating most of the work we did in Chapter 6) or MongoDB, for example. Spring Data gives us convenient and powerful access to standard access mechanisms, including pagination, and saves us from ever having to write manual data access objects again, should we find such things unpleasant.

CHAPTER 8

Showing Your Spring Application on the Web

In the last two chapters, we took a look at persistence in Spring, through the use of JDBCTemplate (when we built our own DAO) and Spring Data (where we let Spring build out all of the mechanisms by which we interacted with a data store). In this chapter, we're going to switch gears and take a look at exposing our application over the World Wide Web, using a templating engine known as Thymeleaf,[1] using Spring Boot's web starter mechanism.

This chapter uses the same source code for data storage as Chapter 7. To build it, you can literally copy the src/main directory from Chapter 7, changing the packages from c07 to c08. There are ways we could have used Chapter 7's classes directly without copying, but since we're trying to keep a flat, short package structure, it's more work than its worth, and explaining Gradle project interdependencies isn't what this chapter is about.

Note   This is a very simple chapter. We're actually not going to cover every real-world aspect of web applications in Spring: no security, no real error handling, and no data validation for writing new data into the database, among other things. These topics are, of course, *important* – but they're also outside of the scope of *this* book. We're going to cover writing data in Chapter 9, but for users interested in writing more complete web applications with Spring, https://apress.com has references that can guide you into in-depth tutorials and references.

First, let's take a look at the build script.

---

[1] Thymeleaf's home page is www.thymeleaf.org/.

© Felipe Gutierrez, Joseph B. Ottinger 2022
F. Gutierrez and J. B. Ottinger, *Introducing Spring Framework 6*, https://doi.org/10.1007/978-1-4842-8637-1_8

Listing 8-1. chapter08/build.gradle

```
plugins {
    id "application"
    id 'org.springframework.boot' version '3.0.0-M3'
    id 'io.spring.dependency-management' version '1.0.12.RELEASE'
}

dependencies {
    implementation \
    'org.springframework.boot:spring-boot-starter-web'
    implementation \
     'org.springframework.boot:spring-boot-starter-thymeleaf'
    implementation \
     'org.springframework.boot:spring-boot-starter-data-jpa'
    implementation \
     'com.h2database:h2:2.1.214'
    testImplementation \
      "org.springframework.boot:spring-boot-starter-test"
    testImplementation \
      "org.testng:testng:$testNgVersion"

}

application {
    mainClass.set("c08.Chapter8")
}
```

We've included a database – H2 – and the spring-boot-starter-data-jpa dependencies, just like in Chapter 7. We've also included spring-boot-starter-web – which gives us the ability to set up HTTP endpoints to connect to – and spring-boot-starter-thymeleaf, which imports our templating engine (Thymeleaf) and sets up the rendering from Spring.

If you've copied the files from Chapter 7 (and moved them to the c08 package instead of c07), your directory tree will look like this:

Listing 8-2. The Directory Structure for Chapter 8 So Far

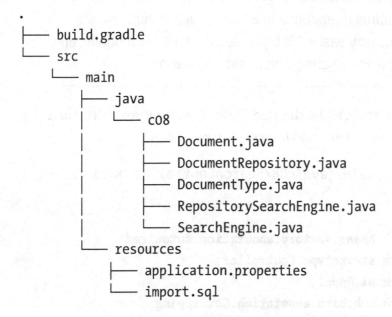

```
.
├── build.gradle
└── src
    └── main
        ├── java
        │   └── c08
        │       ├── Document.java
        │       ├── DocumentRepository.java
        │       ├── DocumentType.java
        │       ├── RepositorySearchEngine.java
        │       └── SearchEngine.java
        └── resources
            ├── application.properties
            └── import.sql
```

Warning   You **must** copy the files from Chapter 7 to Chapter 8's project directory! If you don't, this chapter simply won't work.

A `Controller` in Spring is a type of component, much like a `Repository` is. It maps requests from the HTTP URL into method calls. What we're going to do is map a `SearchController` to "/search" and implement a single mapping after that to "all" – so you can invoke a method, once everything is wired and working, with `http://localhost:8080/search/all`.

The endpoint itself populates a *model* (which is passed in by Spring). A `Model` is just a collection of attributes – represented as a `Map<K,V>` – that gets passed to a rendering engine. After the model is populated, the method returns a path to a template, a resource, that is appropriate for the rendering engine in question; for us, it will be an HTML document with Thymeleaf tags to pull data from the model.

121

> **Note**   This is the "model-view-controller" paradigm in motion: the "controller" populates a "model" and returns a reference to a "view," and it helps isolate the functions of the endpoint very easily. It's highly testable, highly modular, and horribly popular and useful, if you're doing server-side rendering.[2]

Let's take a look at the Controller, and then we'll take a detour through Thymeleaf a bit and cover some more internationalization topics while we're at it.

Listing 8-3. chapter08/src/main/java/c08/SearchController.java

```java
package c08;

import org.springframework.beans.factory.annotation.Autowired;
import org.springframework.stereotype.Controller;
import org.springframework.ui.Model;
import org.springframework.web.bind.annotation.GetMapping;
import org.springframework.web.bind.annotation.RequestMapping;

@Controller
@RequestMapping("/search")
public class SearchController {
  private SearchEngine engine;

  @Autowired
  public void setEngine(SearchEngine engine) {
    this.engine = engine;
  }

  @GetMapping(value = "/all")
  public String searchAll(Model model) {
    model.addAttribute("docs", engine.listAll());
    return "search/all";
  }
}
```

---

[2] It's worth noting that server-side rendering is not very popular; modern UI programming at the time of writing is more likely to use React with REST endpoints than server-side rendering. With that said, the MVC model is a foundational concept and we'll cover REST in a later chapter.

Everything here is fairly normal for Spring so far: we have declared the SearchController as a Controller, so the configuration can pick it up easily, and we provided a mutator so Spring can set the SearchEngine.

The searchAll() method receives a Model reference and simply puts an attribute in the model, called "docs," with the values returned by the listAll() method of the SearchEngine – which, as we saw from the previous chapter, returns all of the entities specified in import.sql.

Then the searchAll() returns a reference to a template, with a value of search/all, which presumably uses the model to render output appropriately. This is *not* a filesystem reference, although it *can* be, and we're going to use a template engine that locates a resource in the classpath using search/all as a location. We'll get there. For now, though, we can easily write a test that executes the SearchController's methods manually and examine their output.

Listing 8-4. chapter08/src/test/java/c08/ControllerTest.java

```java
package c08;

import org.springframework.validation.support.BindingAwareModelMap;
import org.testng.annotations.Test;

import java.util.List;

import static org.testng.Assert.*;

public class ControllerTest {
  @Test
  public void testSearchController() {
    var engine=new SearchEngine() {
      // left empty because we don't use it in the controller.
      @Override
      public List<Document> findByType(DocumentType documentType) {
        return null;
      }

      @Override
      public List<Document> listAll() {
        return List.of(new Document());
      }
    };
```

```
var controller=new SearchController();
var model=new BindingAwareModelMap();
controller.setEngine(engine);

var view=controller.searchAll(model);

@SuppressWarnings("unchecked")
List<Document> docs= (List<Document>) model.getAttribute("docs");

assertNotNull(docs);
assertEquals(docs.size(),1);
assertEquals(view, "search/all");
  }
}
```

An interesting aspect of this test is that it doesn't use Spring at all, except for the
BindingAwareModelMap; it doesn't use any other Spring resources or a Spring context at
all. This is a straightforward Java test that creates a local SearchEngine implementation,
then instantiates a controller, injects our mock SearchEngine, and then invokes the
searchAll() method and examines its output to validate that it matches our expectations.

But how might one use the SearchController on the actual Web? Let's see.

Thymeleaf

Thymeleaf is a template rendering library. The general concept is that you provide a
template – for example, an ordinary HTML page – and a model, and Thymeleaf will
replace content in the template as you direct, using namespaced tags.

Note   We've seen using namespaces in our XML configurations: they're tags like
<context:property-placeholder />, for example. Namespaces allow us
to reuse names by specifying where those names are sourced; for property-
placeholder, it's the context namespace.

The nice thing about the Thymeleaf templates, when they're HTML, is that they are literally valid HTML; the use of the Thymeleaf-specific aspects doesn't matter until Thymeleaf is used to render the template. Thus, you can design an HTML page as a static page until it looks suitable for your purposes and then replace content with Thymeleaf as needed.

Further, in Spring, Thymeleaf integration comes fully ready for internationalization. Spring loads a property bundle called `messages` for us automatically, so we don't have to figure out where something is located, and therefore we can use internationalized text with very little effort.

A template with a name like `search/all` defaults to being located in the classpath under `templates`, so for our Thymeleaf template, we'll want a resource in the classpath at `templates/search/all.html`. We'll need to create the `src/main/resources/templates/search` directory for this.

Listing 8-5. `chapter08/src/main/resources/templates/search/all.html`

```
<!DOCTYPE html>
<html xmlns:th="http://www.thymeleaf.org"
      th:with="lang=${#locale.language}"
      th:lang="${lang}">
<head>
    <title th:text="#{title}">My Documents</title>
</head>
<body style="font-family: verdana sans-serif;">
<h2>
    <span th:text="#{title}">My Documents</span> -
    <span th:text="#{titles.search}">Search</span>
</h2>
<table>
    <thead>
    <tr>
        <th th:text="#{titles.name}">Name</th>
        <th th:text="#{titles.type}">Type</th>
        <th th:text="#{titles.location}">Location</th>
    </tr>
    </thead>
```

```
<tbody>
<tr th:each="doc: ${docs}">
    <td th:text="${doc.name}">First Document</td>
    <td th:text="${doc.type}">PDF</td>
    <td th:text="${doc.location}">/Documents/First.pdf</td>
</tr>
</tbody>
</table>
</body>
</html>
```

Note how it's a "regular HTML page." We declare a namespace of th for Thymeleaf, but the th: tags don't prevent us from being able to open the page in any regular browser for layout.

Note   This page is not laid out particularly well; in the annals of "good web design," this page would probably stand out as something to avoid.

Now we can look at the Thymeleaf rendering. The html block not only declares the namespace for Thymeleaf but also declares with and lang tags. Those are special Thymeleaf *attributes* that target specific HTML attributes. The with attribute allows us to define a variable for later use; what we're doing here is extracting a variable for the template, called lang, based on the language in our rendering environment. The lang attribute then uses this lang *value* to tell the browser what primary language the template is being rendered with, and many browsers can offer you automatic translation to different languages based on this value.

The rendered values use an *expression language*.

In general, the octothorpe – or "pound sign," the # character – is a property interpolation. It will look up a property name and use that as the value for the attribute.

The dollar sign – the $ character – retrieves a value from the template model.

The th:text attribute will replace the value of the current node, such that any placeholder text (the default text as shown in our HTML file) is discarded by the renderer. Thus, if we have a property called hello.text in our resource bundles with a value of "Hello, world" and we want to render the following template block:

```
<span th:text="#{hello.text}">Hi there!</span>
```

This will be rendered by Thymeleaf at runtime as

```
<span>Hello, world</span>
```

We also see the use of `th:each` in our template, which allows us to iterate through *each* element in a collection from our model (the `docs` collection, based on our `SearchController`), using a local name called `doc` for each element. Thus, if we have a list of `Document` types, we can get the name of a given document by using `th:text="${doc.name}"`, which will try to call the `getName()` method of the object being referred to by "doc."

Thymeleaf can be extraordinarily powerful, as with many other templating engines. We are barely scratching the surface of the rendering engine; what we're seeing here is sufficient for our paltry needs, but you may want to browse `www.thymeleaf.org/documentation.html` for more details, especially about the expression language. (Thymeleaf can use Spring's innate expression language if we so desire, for example, or it can use a *completely custom* expression language should you wish to write one.)

As you can see from Listing 8-5, we're using both kinds of expressions – property and model – and let's fill out our property values. We have five property references – `title`, `titles.search`, `titles.name`, and so forth – so those will be our property values in the `messages` bundle, which will be placed in `src/main/resources`. Let's define a few, in rapid order: one for English (the default), one for Spanish, and one for Dutch.

Listing 8-6. `chapter08/src/main/resources/messages.properties`

```
title=My Documents
titles.search=Search
titles.name=Name
titles.type=Type
titles.location=Location
```

Listing 8-7. `chapter08/src/main/resources/messages_es.properties`

```
title=Mis Documentos
titles.search=Buscar
titles.name=Nombre
titles.type=Tipo
titles.location=Ubicacion
```

Listing 8-8. `chapter08/src/main/resources/messages_nl.properties`

```
title=Mijn documenten
titles.search=Zoeken
titles.name=Naam
titles.type=Type
titles.location=Locatie
```

Now, all that remains is to make it so that we can specify the locale for the rendering engine, which is part of our Spring configuration.

Tying It All Together

So far, we've copied our data access code nearly verbatim from Chapter 7, which gives us a working data model; we've built a `Controller` that invokes a rendered page with our data model (including a test), and we've built a Thymeleaf template (ready for internationalization) for use by our controller.

It's time we built a configuration and ran our code. We're going to do it with a class called `Chapter8`.

As a Spring Boot application, the responsibilities of our application class are rather light, overall. Mostly it will declare itself as an application and tell Spring to find its components on the classpath.

The exception to the automation of everything, though, is in the internationalization, which works well, but we'd like to be able to control it.

To handle the internationalization, we need to have a locale resolver and a change interceptor. These will allow us to add `?lang=es` to the URL, for example, to set the locale for the rendering engine (and set a cookie for future invocations, which can be overridden by using the parameter again.) The use of `lang` shows up in our HTML template (as "`th:lang="${lang}`" in the `html` block) and *must* match the attribute name the controller sets – after all, it's part of the model for Thymeleaf.

But with that said, the language resolution is the bulk of our application source code. Let's take a look:

Listing 8-9. chapter08/src/main/java/c08/Chapter8.java

```java
package c08;

import org.springframework.boot.SpringApplication;
import org.springframework.boot.autoconfigure.SpringBootApplication;
import org.springframework.context.annotation.Bean;
import org.springframework.data.jpa.repository.config.
EnableJpaRepositories;
import org.springframework.web.servlet.LocaleResolver;
import org.springframework.web.servlet.config.annotation.Intercepto
rRegistry;
import org.springframework.web.servlet.config.annotation.WebMvcConfigurer;
import org.springframework.web.servlet.i18n.CookieLocaleResolver;
import org.springframework.web.servlet.i18n.LocaleChangeInterceptor;

import java.util.Locale;

@EnableJpaRepositories
@SpringBootApplication
public class Chapter8 implements WebMvcConfigurer {
  @Bean
  public LocaleResolver localeResolver() {
    var localeResolver = new CookieLocaleResolver();
    localeResolver.setDefaultLocale(Locale.US);
    return localeResolver;
  }

  @Bean
  public LocaleChangeInterceptor localeChangeInterceptor() {
    var lci = new LocaleChangeInterceptor();
    lci.setParamName("lang");
    return lci;
  }

  @Override
  public void addInterceptors(InterceptorRegistry registry) {
    registry.addInterceptor(localeChangeInterceptor());
  }
```

```
public static void main(String[] args) {
  SpringApplication.run(Chapter8.class, args);
  }
}
```

At this point, we can run Chapter 8 as an application. If we're in the `chapter08` directory, it's as simple as the following:

```
gradle run
```

If we're in the top-level directory (the directory that *contains* the `chapter08` project directory), we can invoke `run` on the project itself:

```
gradle chapter08:run
```

In all cases, the application should start spewing logs, with the last one containing the following:

```
Started Chapter8 in 2.688 seconds (process running for 2.961)
```

(Your data will obviously vary based on your system and system load.)

Now we can actually open a web browser and check out our application. In Figure 8-1, we see an invocation with no language option (the default, English for your author), from `http://localhost:8080/search/all`:

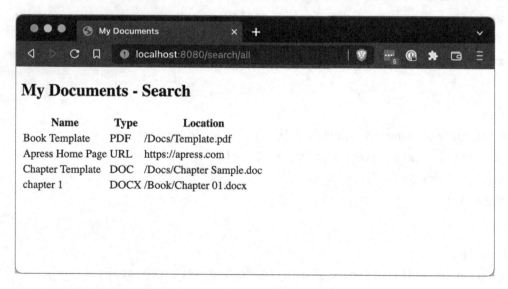

Figure 8-1. *The Search Page in English*

We can switch languages, by adding `?lang=es` on the URL, to `http://localhost:8080/search/all?lang=es`, in Figure 8-2:

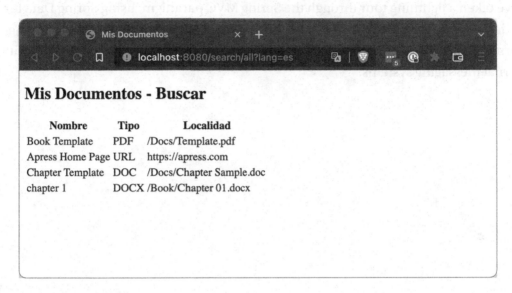

Figure 8-2. *The Search Page in Spanish*

And we can even show off our mastery of Google Translate for the Dutch translation, with `http://localhost:8080/search/all?lang=nl`, as shown in Figure 8-3:

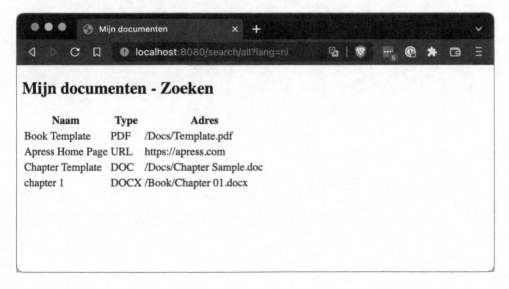

Figure 8-3. *The Search Page in Dutch*

Summary

We've taken a lightning tour through the Spring MVC paradigm, using Spring Data for our data access (the model) and Thymeleaf for the presentation (the view), including internationalization to a light degree. In our next chapter, we're going to integrate with external messaging systems.

PART III

Advanced Techniques with Spring Framework

CHAPTER 9

Integrating Your Spring Application with External Systems

In previous chapters, we've focused on processes that are *synchronous processes* – we issue a command to a database and get a response, or we make a web request, and it gives us a rendered page. In this chapter, we're going to introduce *asynchronous processing*, processes that do not create an immediate response.

We're also going to change approach slightly. In prior chapters, we've been building a "search engine" app, but the result is a lot of duplicated code, much of which isn't relevant to the subject matter we're addressing in a given chapter. We're still going to duplicate *some* code, but we're going to start trimming the scope of the "application" down, to save space and to focus on the specific techniques we're addressing. Readers should be able to easily integrate the new topics into a wider codebase without much effort.

Asynchronous processes are highly useful in computing, because they remove *time pressure* from responses, by their very nature. An HTTP request, for example, might need to respond in 10 milliseconds, or else the user might perceive the app as being "laggy" or slow. That can be difficult to address, because the web *client* is requesting data from a specific server, and that server can be presumed to have finite resources. If it's a busy shopping day, and the consumers are hitting the web server with 400 requests more per second than it was designed to handle, you're going to have a lot of unhappy customers, and fixing that problem isn't trivial.

With asynchronous processing, what typically happens is that each request gets put into a queue, and processes watch that queue for requests; if the queue gets backed up (because the things that watch the queue aren't fast enough), then you simply add

© Felipe Gutierrez, Joseph B. Ottinger 2022
F. Gutierrez and J. B. Ottinger, *Introducing Spring Framework 6*, https://doi.org/10.1007/978-1-4842-8637-1_9

more watchers. If the queue empties, you can then reduce the number of watchers, to minimize resource consumption.

In Chapter 6, we looked at the `JdbcTemplate` class as our gateway to working directly with JDBC (before introducing more flexible mechanisms using Spring Data). The reason we looked at `JdbcTemplate`, even though few programmers should target it directly without specific need, is because the templating model turns out to be quite applicable in other contexts, such as asynchronous programming.

The Process

We're going to use the Java Message Service (JMS) as our example. There are other messaging APIs, but the good news for us is that while they do have slightly different specifics compared to JMS, we can switch to them without changing our architectural approach. JMS is, incidentally, a generalized messaging API itself; we might be using a messaging transport like AMQP 1.0, AMQP 0.9, or MQTT even though we're using JMS as our access layer.

We're going to use the `spring-boot-starter-artemis` project to provide our JMS layer; this actually imports the `spring-messaging` and `spring-jms` modules and wraps functionality around them, in particular around the Artemis message broker. If we include `artemis-jms-server` as a project dependency, Spring will start up a broker for us if one isn't already available, much as the Spring Data relational dependencies will embed a database for us.

Artemis[1] is one of many message brokers, based on the HornetQ message broker contributed to the Apache project. It provides a JMS-compatible container, of course, but also provides AMQP 1.0 and MQTT as underlying protocols. We're going to focus on JMS, as it's the most generic messaging layer.

Note   The most important thing we can learn is the general *technique* of using asynchronous messaging. If you use AMQP 0.9 (i.e., RabbitMQ), or MQTT, or any other supported messaging specification, the techniques will change only in terms of the specific annotations used, if you need specific broker features.

---

[1] Artemis' home page is `https://activemq.apache.org/components/artemis/`.

As with JDBC, the key interface for JMS is `JmsTemplate`. In real-world applications, it's used primarily for *writing* messages, although it has mechanisms for receiving messages as well. (We'll be using annotations to set up message listeners rather than leveraging `JmsTemplate` for receiving messages, as this is far more convenient and common for application developers.)

The key method for sending messages is `send()`, oddly enough, with a few variants. The most useful one is `send(String destinationName, MessageCreator messageCreator)`, which allows us to send a `Message` to a specific destination on the fly.

Let's start building out an application so we can see how this works.

Our "application" is going to be a simple one. We're going to create an application that sends 20 documents to an asynchronous queue; that queue will have a listener that creates database records based on those documents. We're also going to dump the database contents after a few seconds, to make sure the data was written as we expected it to be.

Let's start building this out, by looking at our `build.gradle`, first.

Listing 9-1. `chapter09/build.gradle`

```
plugins {
    id "application"
    id 'org.springframework.boot' version '3.0.0-M4'
    id 'io.spring.dependency-management' version '1.0.13.RELEASE'
}

dependencies {
    implementation  \
      'org.springframework.boot:spring-boot-starter-data-jpa'
    implementation  \
      'org.springframework.boot:spring-boot-starter-artemis'
    implementation  \
      'com.h2database:h2:2.1.214'
    // implementation  \
    //   'org.apache.activemq:artemis-jms-server:2.24.0'
}

application {
    mainClass.set("md.MyDocsApp")
}
```

The important things to note here are:

1. The use of `spring-boot-starter-artemis`, which provides the JMS libraries for our application classpath, as well as providing hooks to start Artemis for us if we need it

2. The inclusion of `artemis-jms-server`, which is required if we want Boot to instantiate our broker for us (and we do, because broker configuration is very simple in development but in actual environments can be very complex and is outside of the scope of this book)

3. The inclusion of a database (H2) and the `spring-boot-starter-data-jpa` dependency, which gives us database access

Now let's get the database access out of the way. We will have a very simple Document class, with `toString()` implemented so we can trivially see the values in the Document for output. We're using Spring Data JPA, so it has the JPA annotations included. Note that this class *must* implement Serializable, because we're going to literally be serializing and deserializing it through our message broker.

Listing 9-2. `chapter09/src/main/java/md/Document.java`

```
package md;

import jakarta.persistence.*;

import java.io.Serializable;
import java.util.StringJoiner;

@Entity
@Table(name="document")
public class Document implements Serializable {
  @Id
  @GeneratedValue(strategy = GenerationType.AUTO)
  Integer id;
  @Column(nullable = false)
  String name;
  @Column(nullable = false)
  String location;
```

```java
  Document() {
  }
  Document(String name, String location) {
    setName(name);
    setLocation(location);
  }
  public Integer getId() {
    return id;
  }

  public void setId(Integer id) {
    this.id = id;
  }

  public String getName() {
    return name;
  }

  public void setName(String name) {
    this.name = name;
  }

  public String getLocation() {
    return location;
  }

  public void setLocation(String location) {
    this.location = location;
  }

  @Override
  public String toString() {
    return new StringJoiner(", ", Document.class.getSimpleName() + "[", "]")
      .add("id=" + id)
      .add("name='" + name + "'")
      .add("location='" + location + "'")
      .toString();
  }
}
```

We also need a `DocumentRepository` to manage the interaction with a database for Document:

Listing 9-3. chapter09/src/main/java/md/DocumentRepository.java

```
package md;

import org.springframework.data.repository.CrudRepository;

public interface DocumentRepository
  extends CrudRepository<Document, Integer> {
}
```

> **Note**   This is a *very* stripped-down interface, as we are doing no querying or unusual access in this chapter. However, there's absolutely nothing preventing you from adding any features as you see fit.

We still want to make sure that our schema is created when our application starts up, so we need an `application.properties` file to tell Hibernate to create the database. In production, this is a bad idea – you want to control your database schema very carefully – but for our sample apps in this book, we want the implicit creation of our schema.

Listing 9-4. chapter09/src/main/main/resources/application.properties

```
spring.jpa.properties.hibernate.hbm2ddl.auto=create
```

We have three classes left to create: `JmsPublisher`, which will *publish* our data to a JMS queue, `JmsReceiver`, which will *receive* the data from the queue (which shouldn't surprise you, given the name), and lastly, a `MyDocsApp`, which will manage the configuration and coordination of tasks.

> **Note**   Your author would prefer `JMSReceiver` over `JmsReceiver`, personally. There are ongoing arguments over naming standards when acronyms are involved; is it `DvdPlayer` or `DVDPlayer`? I fall on the `DVDPlayer` side, but Spring chose `JmsTemplate` over `JMSTemplate`, and thus I am conforming to *that* standard instead of my own. I am a team player, after all.

Let's take a look at `JmsReceiver` first.

Listing 9-5. chapter09/src/main/java/md/JmsReceiver.java

```java
package md;

import org.springframework.jms.annotation.JmsListener;
import org.springframework.stereotype.Component;

@Component
public class JmsReceiver {
  DocumentRepository dao;

  JmsReceiver(DocumentRepository dao) {
    this.dao = dao;
  }

  @JmsListener(destination = "documents")
  public void receiveMessage(Document document) {
    System.out.println("Received <" + document + ">");
    this.dao.save(document);
  }
}
```

This is a fundamentally simple class. It uses a `DocumentRepository`; thus, it uses one supplied to the constructor, but the interesting part is the `receiveMessage` method, annotated with `JmsListener`. The `JmsListener` annotation here uses a queue named `"documents"` – a sort of "named mailbox," if you will, and specified with the `destination` attribute of the `@JmsListener` annotation – and it expects the "payload" of the message to be a `Document` reference.

We're not really doing anything here to coerce the payload type. As we'll see in our `JmsPublisher`, we're sending a `Document` in serial form (thus, it's the right type, no matter what); you can always instruct Spring to attempt to convert an incoming message to a valid type as required, with a `MessageConverter`.

> **Note**   We're not configuring the `MessageConverter` here because we're still trying to avoid broker configuration. There are simply too many options and alternatives to discuss some without acknowledging the rest of them, and that could easily double the length of this *book*, not to mention hiding the purpose of this *chapter*.

Once we receive the `Document`, we display it – just to show that we have it – and then use the `DocumentRepository save()` method, which is responsible for talking to the database.

This method is fundamentally simple, but the complexity of the operation is *completely* malleable. If the mechanism for saving a document needed to talk to an external service to validate ISBN for a book, or do some expensive validation based on the document type, or *any other process we need*, the entry point for the service remains the same; we just add whatever processing we happen to need for our application requirements.

What's more, the performance impact of the entry point is (nearly) irrelevant, because of the asynchronous invocation. If we can only process one `Document` at a time in a given virtual machine, for some reason, all we need to do to increase our throughput is simply add another JVM or another. As long as the limit isn't based on something external to our process, we can increase the number of `Document` listeners arbitrarily.

> **Note**   Of course, if the limit is external to our consumer, we might not be able to change the throughput quite as trivially. Imagine that our validation uses a web service that has a limit of one process at a time; if we send 17 requests through, that limit of one-at-a-time is still going to be what limits our processing as well. Welcome to the world of asynchronous architecture.

Let's take a look at what "feeds" the `JmsReceiver` – the `JmsPublisher`.

Listing 9-6. `chapter09/src/main/java/md/JmsPublisher.java`

```java
package md;

import org.springframework.jms.core.JmsTemplate;
import org.springframework.stereotype.Component;

@Component
```

```java
public class JmsPublisher {
  private final JmsTemplate jmsTemplate;

  public JmsPublisher(JmsTemplate jmsTemplate) {
    this.jmsTemplate = jmsTemplate;
  }

  public void send(Document document) {
    jmsTemplate.send("documents",
      session -> session.createObjectMessage(document));
  }
}
```

This is yet another very simple class. It receives a `JmsTemplate`, because that's how it publishes to a named queue, in the `send()` method. That method mostly wraps the `JmsTemplate.send()` method, using a `MessageCreator` lambda to create a JMS `ObjectMessage` with the `Document`.

Most senders will follow the same structure; the only variations would be in the destination names (`"documents"`, here) and in possibly the structure of the `Message`; it's an `ObjectMessage` in this case (because we control the sender and the receiver, and we can use the serialized form), but you might use a `TextMessage` or some other type of `Message` implementation depending on your needs. (If you needed to send a message in JSON or XML, for example, a `TextMessage` would be a good choice, but then you'd convert the `Document` to JSON or XML, as required, as part of the message creation.)

Now we have working (and simple) classes to *consume* messages (the `JmsReceiver`) and *produce* messages (the `JmsPublisher`) – it's time to tie everything together into an application of sorts.

Our application will have two `CommandLineRunner` beans as part of its configuration.

The first `CommandLineRunner` will require a `JmsPublisher` – which Spring will provide automatically, of course, since it's an available `Component` – and publish 20 `Document` instances, each with a random UUID.[2]

---

[2] Why do we use UUID instead of the ranged value? Because readers might want to run one, four, or a hundred instances of the application at once. Using the ranged values would duplicate the names, whereas random UUIDs, as shown here, won't conflict with each other. So, reader, if you so desire, run as many copies of this application as you like. It'd be fun.

The second CommandLineRunner will wait 2 seconds[3] – plenty of time for our publishing cycle to run – and dump *every* Document our database has to the console, as a simple check that data *was* written to the database.

Here's our simple MyDocsApp class:

Listing 9-7. chapter09/src/main/java/md/MyDocsApp.java

```
package md;

import org.springframework.boot.CommandLineRunner;
import org.springframework.boot.SpringApplication;
import org.springframework.boot.autoconfigure.SpringBootApplication;
import org.springframework.context.annotation.Bean;
import
org.springframework.data.jpa.repository.config.EnableJpaRepositories;
import org.springframework.jms.annotation.EnableJms;

import java.util.UUID;
import java.util.stream.IntStream;

@EnableJpaRepositories
@EnableJms
@SpringBootApplication
public class MyDocsApp {
  public static void main(String[] args) {
    SpringApplication.run(MyDocsApp.class, args);
  }

  @Bean
  CommandLineRunner send(JmsPublisher publisher) {
    return args -> {
      IntStream.rangeClosed(1, 20).forEach(
        (value) -> {
```

---

[3] "Why does the database dump wait two whole seconds?" is an obvious question to ask – and it's a good question. The real answer is to allow enough time for readers to start other copies of the application, as mentioned in the prior footnote, although they'd still have to be quick about it – 2 seconds is enough time to give you room to run another application without taking so much time that it feels like nothing is happening. Feel free to play with the delay to fit your needs.

```java
        var uuid=UUID.randomUUID().toString();
        publisher.send(
          new Document(
            "document " + uuid,
            "/documents/doc" + uuid
          ));
      }
    );
  };
}

@Bean
CommandLineRunner summarize(DocumentRepository dao) {
  return args->{
    Thread.sleep(2000);
    for(var document:dao.findAll()) {
      System.out.println(document);
    }
  };
}
}
```

We can run this with `gradle :chapter09:run`, and it emits a bunch of messages about receiving (and storing) a bunch of documents and then displays the documents stored in the database so we can validate that we've sent (and received) messages through the broker.

So what have we seen in this code?

1. We've seen how to set up dependencies for use of asynchronous processing in Spring 6, focusing on JMS. Using a different API would be a matter of changing the specific annotations and dependencies, but the *pattern* would be the same. A broker will be started up for us if one isn't already running, a situation ideal for development because it means that the developers don't have to go through the process of setting up a broker.

2. We've seen how to create listeners that listen on destinations.

3. We've seen how to create components that can publish *to* destinations.

4. We've seen how to use the publishing components to write to those destinations, in a class that might serve as a template for bulk data upload.

Summary

This chapter has been a whirlwind introduction to using asynchronous messaging APIs in Spring, leveraging the JMS integration within the Artemis message broker, specifically to expose the ability to save data through our data access object asynchronously. Other messaging APIs are available to Spring and work in similar fashion to the JMS integration, but we've barely scratched the surface of an entire architectural approach that has surprising power for scalability.

In our next chapter, we're going to switch gears again and look at the Web again, by exposing REST functionality to our data access object.

CHAPTER 10

Exposing a REST API

In our last chapter, we saw how to use asynchronous messaging APIs in Spring using the `JmsTemplate` to send messages and the `@JmsReceiver` annotation to *receive* them. Now we're going to step back into the land of the Web, to build a set of endpoints that expose our data model to a rich client, using REST.

What Is REST?

REST stands for "REpresentational State Transfer" and generally refers to APIs that conform to a rough definition of resources accessed via URLs directly. It was defined by Dr. Roy Fielding in a rather well-known dissertation.[1]

In general, REST asserts that every *thing* in your model can be represented through a URL, and HTTP verbs can be used to interact with those things. For example, to get a `Document` with an id of 1, one might access with an HTTP GET, at a URL of `http://yourhost.com/documents/1`. To access *all* documents, you might *get* `http://yourhost.com/documents` – note the lack of the identifier. Also note that `documents` are referred to as plural; you're not accessing *a document*, but you're accessing one of a *set* of documents.

To create a `Document`, one could use a POST to `http://yourhost.com/documents` – as you're creating a new `Document`, you have no `id` value, so you're posting the new values to the collection of documents.

---

[1] Dr. Fielding's dissertation can be found at `www.ics.uci.edu/~fielding/pubs/dissertation/top.htm`, and it's quite worth reading.

© Felipe Gutierrez, Joseph B. Ottinger 2022
F. Gutierrez and J. B. Ottinger, *Introducing Spring Framework 6*, https://doi.org/10.1007/978-1-4842-8637-1_10

To *update* a document, you could use HTTP PUT (or perhaps PATCH, but usually PUT in my experience); I've also seen POST used for this purpose, but that's not advised (as it overloads POST for the application in question).[2]

To *delete* a document, the HTTP DELETE verb comes into play, again accessing the specific resource at `http://yourhost.com/documents/1` for a Document with an `id` of 1.

Building a REST API in Spring

In Spring, we can create a controller using the `@Controller` annotation, but `@Controller` implies that the HTTP methods return a *route* – to a rendering engine like Thymeleaf or something similar. In REST, the controller renders *data*, not *a page* – it's meant for machine consumption, not human consumption, generally speaking.

Thus, Spring also gives us a `@RestController` annotation that marks the HTTP methods as rendering an object model as the response body, instead of returning a reference to a route for which a renderer would be responsible.

We return data itself from the methods, not references to routes with a populated `Model`.

This also means that to create an end-user API, a rendering engine would have to be built using ... something. Typically a rich client is built with JavaScript, using React or Angular (or any of a host of other such frameworks), and that rich client calls our REST endpoint to get the data it needs.

Note   JavaScript is outside of this book's scope, and building a rich client well deserves its own book; this is not that book! We're going to stay laser-focused on Spring here, but Apress has many excellent resources for JavaScript development if you are interested.

Let's get started. As always, we'll begin with our project file for Gradle.

---

[2] It's worth noting that REST is a specification full of recommendations, and while most people find the recommendations make sense, not everyone follows every one of them. Each application effectively makes its own independent decisions about how to implement functionality, and most of it will be similar to other REST applications without being exact matches.

Listing 10-1. chapter10/build.gradle

```
plugins {
    id "application"
    id 'org.springframework.boot' version '3.0.0-M3'
    id 'io.spring.dependency-management' version '1.0.11.RELEASE'
}

dependencies {
    implementation \
      'org.springframework.boot:spring-boot-starter-web'
    implementation \
      'org.springframework.boot:spring-boot-starter-data-jpa'
    testImplementation \
      'org.springframework.boot:spring-boot-starter-test'
    implementation \
      'com.h2database:h2:2.1.214'
    testImplementation \
      "org.testng:testng:$testNgVersion"
}

application {
    mainClass.set("md.MyDocsApp")
}
```

So far, there's nothing particularly new here; we're including the Spring Boot starters for JPA and the Web and for testing. We also include TestNG (because that's the test framework we're using) and H2 for our embedded database.

We also need a database entity, a repository, and a configuration to work with. As with Chapter 9, we'll use a simplified database entity, one that ignores the DocumentType enum we've been using:

Listing 10-2. chapter10/src/main/java/md/Document.java

```
package md;

import jakarta.persistence.*;

import java.io.Serializable;
import java.util.StringJoiner;
```

```java
@Entity
@Table(name="document")
public class Document {
  @Id
  @GeneratedValue(strategy = GenerationType.IDENTITY)
  Integer id;
  @Column(nullable = false)
  String name;
  @Column(nullable = false)
  String location;

  public Document() {
  }

  Document(String name, String location) {
    setName(name);
    setLocation(location);
  }

  public Integer getId() {
    return id;
  }

  public void setId(Integer id) {
    this.id = id;
  }

  public String getName() {
    return name;
  }

  public void setName(String name) {
    this.name = name;
  }

  public String getLocation() {
    return location;
  }
```

```
public void setLocation(String location) {
  this.location = location;
}
@Override
public String toString() {
  return String.format(
    "%s[id=%d,name='%s',location='%s']",
    Document.class.getSimpleName(),
    id,
    name,
    location);
}
}
```

Our entity is very standard and simple; it's long, because most of it is boilerplate.

As stated, we also need a DocumentRepository:

Listing 10-3. chapter10/src/main/java/md/DocumentRepository.java

```
package md;

import org.springframework.data.jpa.repository.Query;
import org.springframework.data.repository.CrudRepository;

import java.util.List;

public interface DocumentRepository
  extends CrudRepository<Document, Integer> {
  List<Document> findAll();
  @Query("select max(d.id) from Document d")
  Integer findMaxId();
}
```

The interface for CrudRepository<Document,Integer> actually defines findAll() already, but the signature defaults to Iterable<Document> findAll(). That's not bad, but working with Iterable<Document> is more gruntwork than working with a List<Document>; what we're doing here is telling Spring Data that we want it to use *this* signature instead, and thus findAll() returns a List<Document> instead. We could use a Set<Document> but we want ordered access to the collection, so List<Document> it is.

151

> **Note**   We're coercing the type of findAll() for *convenience*. Using Iterable actually does have advantages, in that it allows different mechanisms for iteration; with Iterable, for example, Spring Data doesn't have to fetch the entire dataset to build the returned reference. With List<Document>, it returns the entire dataset at once, so it's theoretically a slower method call.

We also have a custom query: findMaxId(). This runs a JPQL query to, well, get the highest maximum id the database contains. We'll use this to try to find an id for a Document that doesn't exist in our test code.

Next, we need the "application," which just relies on Spring Boot to load our components for us. We've not gotten to the fun parts of this application yet; we're going to have a DocumentController and three more files for testing, shortly. But here's the last of the basic application's shell code that we need before we get to the interesting bits:

Listing 10-4. chapter10/src/main/java/md/MyDocsApp.java

```java
package md;

import org.springframework.boot.SpringApplication;
import org.springframework.boot.autoconfigure.SpringBootApplication;
import org.springframework.data.jpa.repository.config.EnableJpaRepositories;

@EnableJpaRepositories
@SpringBootApplication
public class MyDocsApp {
  public static void main(String[] args) {
    SpringApplication.run(MyDocsApp.class, args);
  }

}
```

At last, we're ready to take a look at the REST controller itself. For the most part, it's not anything particularly special, except we're still short-circuiting some important architectural aspects.

In typical Spring code, we'd have *three* classes, where our sample has *two*: we have the DocumentController that talks to a DocumentRepository. In most Spring design, you'd have a DocumentController that delegated to a DocumentService, that itself called methods on the DocumentRepository.

So why don't we have *that*? Well, the main reason is because for what we're demonstrating – the REST endpoints – the extra architecture doesn't add anything. The DocumentController would have service.delete(id);, and the DocumentService would defer to the DocumentRepository, and all we'd have is a set of classes that mostly delegated code further down into the architecture.

It's very clean that way, and recommended, but for our purposes *here* all it does is make the chapter longer, for no real benefit.

Note   In your own code, you should prefer the multiple tiers. We're not using them here unless there's a benefit to them, but that doesn't mean there's *no* benefit to them; it's just not beneficial *here*. Instead, we're combining the service and controller layers into one class.

Here's the code, and we'll walk through the significant bits after we see the listing:

Listing 10-5. chapter10/src/main/java/md/DocumentController.java

```java
package md;

import org.springframework.http.HttpStatus;
import org.springframework.transaction.annotation.Transactional;
import org.springframework.web.bind.annotation.*;

import java.util.List;

@ResponseStatus(value = HttpStatus.NOT_FOUND)
class NotFoundException extends RuntimeException {
  NotFoundException(Integer id) {
    super(String.format("resource not found: %d",id));
  }
}
```

```java
@RestController()
public class DocumentController {
  private DocumentRepository dao;

  public DocumentController(DocumentRepository dao) {
    this.dao = dao;
  }

  Document loadDocument(Integer id) {
    var doc = dao.findById(id);
    if (doc.isPresent()) {
      return doc.get();
    }
    throw new NotFoundException(id);
  }

  @GetMapping("documents/{id}")
  @Transactional
  Document get(@PathVariable Integer id) {
    return loadDocument(id);
  }

  @GetMapping("documents")
  @Transactional
  List<Document> getAll() {
    return dao.findAll();
  }

  @PostMapping("documents")
  @Transactional
  Document post(@RequestBody Document document) {
    return dao.save(document);
  }

  @DeleteMapping("documents/{id}")
  @Transactional
  void delete(@PathVariable Integer id) {
```

```
  var document = loadDocument(id);
  dao.deleteById(id);
}

@PutMapping("documents/{id}")
@Transactional
void put(@PathVariable Integer id, @RequestBody Document document) {
  var loadedDocument = loadDocument(id);
  if(id!= document.getId()) {
    throw new NotFoundException(id);
  }
  loadedDocument.setName(document.getName());
  loadedDocument.setLocation(document.getLocation());

  // we don't need an explicit save() because updating a managed
  // entity persists changes when the transaction ends.
  }
}
```

First, let's note the use of a custom exception, the NotFoundException. This exists so we can easily map an exception condition to a specific HTTP code (404, in this case, the "not found" exception), through the use of the @ResponseStatus annotation.

The first thing we see in the DocumentController itself is the use of @RestController instead of @Controller. This means that the method don't return mapping to views (as with @Controller) – the methods return the actual objects we want to render for the client or void if there's no HTTP response body.

Next, we see the declaration of an injected value, the DocumentRepository.

After that, we see the loadDocument() method, which handles the use of Optional<Document> to throw a NotFoundException if the value isn't present. JPA itself actually handles such exceptions fairly trivially, but Spring Data has to compensate for the possible use of other data mechanisms.

If we didn't care about the specific error handling (the assignment of response status as well as a custom message), we could use return dao.findById(id).orElseThrow)⇒new NotFoundException(id)⇒new NotFoundException(id, which would end up with the exception being mapped to an HTTP server error response; this code is a little more clunky than just mapping the exception as we've done.

We want the innate mapping of exceptions like this because "not found" isn't the same as a "server error."

Then we get to the actual mapping of our methods themselves. For methods we access with HTTP GET and other path-related verbs, we have a @PathVariable – thus we can call get(Integer) over the Web by using a URL such as http://localhost:8080/documents/1 to access a Document with an id of 1. As with our @Controller, the @PathVariable is extrapolated from the URL path. The variable name is mapped to the {id} in the path, if there's a match; we could tell the annotation how to map the name specifically if the argument name differed from the name in the URL path.

The HTTP methods are all annotated not only with the appropriate request annotations but with @Transactional, which means that we're establishing barriers around the operations such that they're "safe" – if the database has a problem updating a record, an exception will be thrown and the updates will be properly discarded without leaving your database in a corrupted state. Our data model is too simple to have any real problems with transactions, but it's still good practice.[3]

We have another GET method, except this time without the /{id} path variable; this is how REST suggests to retrieve a *collection*, in our case the entire set of Document objects we're managing.

The other methods are actually pretty straightforward: post() creates a new Document based on the body of the HTTP request sent (via HTTP POST, of course); delete() loads an existing document (throwing an HTTP "not found" response if the id doesn't exist) and then deletes the entity. We do throw away the document reference, but if you wanted to, you could use it to report that the entity was deleted; since it's unused, if you're interested you can just remove the reference altogether.

The put() method is a little more interesting; it's how we *modify* an existing Document. It takes the id from the URL *and* has body content. It then loads the Document (again, throwing a "not found" exception if it doesn't exist on the database) and checks that the loaded document's id matches the "updated document" id, throwing an exception if there's not a match.

It then copies the data from the "updated document" into the entity that was loaded from the database. When the method ends (and the transaction is committed), the database will contain the *new* values rather than the old.

---

[3] If you're wondering, yes, it's slightly ironic that we're using @Transactional as "good practice" in a class that really should delegate to a service class for all transactions.

All this is well and good, and we have a "running application" should we want one – but let's build a test instead.

First, we need to set up an `import.sql` to have a "default set" of Document entities to work with.

Note   None of this is "new" — we've been using similar import mechanisms. Do note, though, that this file is *not quite* the same as the earlier versions of the `import.sql` we've seen; notably, it doesn't include the document ids, because the Document sets the `id` type as being generated as a database identity field. (The exact semantics of this depend on the database in question.)

Listing 10-6. chapter10/src/test/resources/import.sql

```
insert into document (name, location)
values (
        'Book Template',
        '/Docs/Template.pdf'
    );
insert into document (name, location)
values (
        'Apress Home Page',
        'https://apress.com'
    );
insert into document (name, location)
values (
        'Chapter Template',
        '/Docs/Chapter Sample.doc'
    );
insert into document (name, location)
values (
        'chapter 1',
        '/Book/Chapter 01.docx'
    );
```

Since we have embedded newlines in our `import.sql`, we need to have an `application.properties` that tells Hibernate to allow multiple lines for the import:

Listing 10-7. chapter10/src/test/resources/application.properties

```
spring.jpa.properties.hibernate.hbm2ddl\
  .import_files_sql_extractor=org.hibernate\
  .tool.hbm2ddl.MultipleLinesSqlCommandExtractor
```

Now we get to our actual test class itself! There's a lot to unpack, but most of it is pretty straightforward. Let's take a look at the source code and then walk through it:

Listing 10-8. chapter10/src/test/java/md/ControllerTest.java

```java
package md;

import org.springframework.beans.factory.annotation.Autowired;
import org.springframework.boot.test.context.SpringBootTest;
import org.springframework.boot.test.web.client.TestRestTemplate;
import org.springframework.boot.test.web.server.LocalServerPort;
import org.springframework.http.HttpStatus;
import
org.springframework.test.context.testng.AbstractTestNGSpringContextTests;
import org.testng.annotations.Test;

import static org.testng.Assert.assertEquals;

@SpringBootTest(webEnvironment = SpringBootTest.WebEnvironment.RANDOM_PORT)
public class ControllerTest
  extends AbstractTestNGSpringContextTests {
  @LocalServerPort
  private int port;
  @Autowired
  private TestRestTemplate restTemplate;
  @Autowired
  private DocumentRepository dao;

  private String buildUrl() {
    return String.format("http://localhost:%d/documents", port);
  }
```

```java
private Document getFirstDocument() {
  var allDocs = dao.findAll();
  var first = allDocs.get(0);
  return first;
}

private Document getDocument(int id) {
  var resp = restTemplate
    .getForEntity(buildUrl() + "/" + id, Document.class);
  assertEquals(resp.getStatusCode(), HttpStatus.OK);
  return resp.getBody();
}
@Test
void testGetDocument() {
  Document first = getFirstDocument();
  var document = getDocument(first.getId());
  assertEquals(document.getName(), first.getName());
}

@Test
void testGetBadDocument() {
  var highest = dao.findMaxId();
  var resp = restTemplate
    .getForEntity(buildUrl() + "/" + (highest + 1), Document.class);
  assertEquals(resp.getStatusCode(), HttpStatus.NOT_FOUND);
}

@Test
void testGetAllDocuments() {
  var allDocs = dao.findAll();
  var resp = restTemplate
    .getForEntity(buildUrl(), Document[].class);
  var documents = resp.getBody();
  assertEquals(allDocs.size(), documents.length);
}
```

```
@Test
void testPostDocument() {
  // preserve the original list of documents
  var allDocs = dao.findAll();
  var newDocument = new Document("new document", "/new document.docx");
  var resp = restTemplate
    .postForEntity(buildUrl(), newDocument, Document.class);
  var savedDocument = resp.getBody();
  var allDocsAfterPOST = dao.findAll();
  assertEquals(allDocsAfterPOST.size(), allDocs.size() + 1);
}

@Test
void testDeleteDocument() {
  // preserve the original list of documents
  var allDocs = dao.findAll();
  var first = allDocs.get(0);
  restTemplate.delete(buildUrl() + "/" + first.getId());

  var allDocsAfterPOST = dao.findAll();
  assertEquals(allDocsAfterPOST.size(), allDocs.size() - 1);
}

@Test
void testPutDocument() {
  var first = getFirstDocument();
  // we are copying the document over to a new copy
  var updatedDocument = new Document(first.getName(), "/updated
  location");
  updatedDocument.setId(first.getId());
  restTemplate.put(buildUrl() + "/" + first.getId(), updatedDocument);
  var updated = getDocument(first.getId());
  assertEquals(updated.getName(), first.getName());
  assertEquals(updated.getLocation(), "/updated location");
}
```

```
@Test
void testPutDocumentWithBadId() {
  var first = getFirstDocument();
  // we are copying the document over to a new copy
  var updatedDocument = new Document(first.getName(), "/another
  location");

  // mangle the id.
  updatedDocument.setId(first.getId()+1);

  restTemplate.put(buildUrl() + "/" + first.getId(), updatedDocument);

  // it should be the same entity: no changes applied
  var updated = getDocument(first.getId());
  assertEquals(updated.getName(), first.getName());
  assertEquals(updated.getLocation(), "/updated location");
 }

}
```

In addition to being a long source file, there's a lot to unpack! Let's start at the top. First, we have a @SpringBootTest annotation, and we are setting the webEnvironment value to SpringBootTest.WebEnvironment.RANDOM_PORT. This will create a server environment for our tests, using a random port (surprised?) – and we can use another annotation, @LocalServerPort, to let Spring know how to provide which port was selected.

The class definition itself is standard for Spring and TestNG; it extends AbstractTestNGSpringContextTests as our other tests have.

We then see the use of @LocalServerPort, which we'll use to construct our URLs.

We also have a TestRestTemplate reference and a reference to our DocumentRepository. TestRestTemplate is a class that doesn't abort on exceptions, which means we can *examine* the exceptions more easily in our tests than if we had to add try/catch blocks to intercept issues.

> **Note**   The use of `TestRestTemplate` implies that there's also a
> `RestTemplate`. This may or may not surprise you, but there *is* a
> `RestTemplate` – and it's used in the same way that `TestRestTemplate` is,
> with the main difference being that `RestTemplate` propagates exceptional
> conditions *as* exceptions instead of just embedding them in response variables. (In
> other words, `TestRestTemplate` preserves exceptions for us to examine, and
> `RestTemplate` throws them. It's simpler to test with `TestRestTemplate`.)

We have three more utility methods: one to build a URL using our port reference, one to get the "first document" out of all of our documents (unsorted, because it's a utility method to get effectively **any** document that exists), and one that uses our `restTemplate` to retrieve a `Document` via REST – it's the first one that we really care about, because it shows how the template works.

It's pretty simple: `getForEntity()` takes a URL and a reference class. Thus, we build a URL to fit the `get()` method in our controller, and we pass in a `Document.class` so the entity type can be mapped. Our utility method also presumes that the request **works** – if the `Document` isn't found, we expect the test to fail, so we use `assertEquals()` to make sure the response code is 200. We then use `getBody()` to get the deserialized content from the response – remember, when we call `getForEntity()` we pass in the type of the content, so the body type will return the deserialized `Document`.

After that, the test methods are pretty straightforward.

The `testGetDocument()` grabs a single `Document` from the list of all `Document` entities directly from the database and then tries to fetch that specific `Document` from the REST endpoint. If the status code is 200 – as validated by `getDocument()` – and the expected name matches, we can assume the GET succeeded and returned the data we expected.

The `testGetBadDocument()` is a little more interesting. The very first thing it does is find the highest `id` in the database. It then tries to get the *next* id (which shouldn't exist[4])

---

[4] There's something wrong with this test! This is not meant to be an exhaustive example, but the test is *not* transactional; it's possible that we could get the maximum id, and *then* another process could create a new `Document` (which would get the "next id," one higher than the "maximum"), and then we'd fetch the "missing document" using the id that was *just* allocated. We could create a service that established better transactional boundaries to make this test a little stronger, but to make it truly rigorous would be a lot of work from which most users wouldn't learn much. So we're going to make the "safe assumption" that no extra applications just *happen* to be hitting our random port at *just* the wrong time.

and checks the response's status code to make sure it's a 404. If it isn't a 404, we expect the test to fail.

The `testGetAllDocuments()` method uses a `Document[].class` as the return type. We could have used a `List<Document>` if we were willing to create a new type that Java could use to figure out that the `List` held `Document` references (remember, Java doesn't reify, so to the compiled code `List<Document>` is the same as `List`); in this case, an array has the same semantics (in that it has a length) that we can compare against the size of the list of *all* documents that we retrieve at the beginning of the method.

Note   So why did we use a `Document[]` instead of a `List<Document>`? Because of the reification! When the REST endpoint returns the set of `Document` entities, it does so in a JSON list, and when we invoke `getForEntity()`, we don't have a reified type for `List<Document>` – so we'd have to cast or use some other workaround. A JSON array can be used for both a `List<?>` and an array, so we used the array for simplicity's sake.

After that, we have the `testPostDocument()` method, which checks to make sure that the list of `Document` entities after the `POST` is one greater than the list *before* the `POST`.

The `testDeleteDocument()` method inverts that process; it deletes one document and validates that the set of all documents is smaller than it was.

Lastly, we have two tests for `PUT`: `testPutDocument()`, which – logically enough – tests that we can apply updates to an existing document, making sure the update was applied to the database, and then `testPutDocumentWithBadId()`, which submits a changed `Document` with a new `id` as well. `PUT` doesn't return a meaningful response from the `RestTemplate`, so we check against the database directly to make sure no updates were applied.

Most of these are fairly straightforward; they're not exhaustive, but they're "complete enough" that if the `DocumentController` is implemented improperly, our tests will fail. It'd be a good exercise for the reader to make the tests more thorough, but it wouldn't help demonstrate anything new about the API we're building.

Summary

What we've seen in this chapter is the use of `@RestController` to create a simpler endpoint for rendering data for rich clients, as well as some extra features of Spring Data (like the ability to save entities). We've also seen a testing mechanism that goes through our controller to validate that the REST endpoints work; we have a model by which we can build a client to exercise document creation, reads, updates, and deletes (but ironically, not searches, but given that we have implemented a *controller*, merging our `SearchEngine` code from earlier chapters would not be difficult *at all*. It'd just serve as the service layer, delegated to by the controller.)

In our next chapter, we're going to switch gears again and look at how we can send and receive email in Spring.

CHAPTER 11

Sending Emails from Within Spring

In this chapter, we're going to look at sending and receiving email in Spring. We're also going to look at a way that we can *schedule* processes in Spring such that they don't block an executing thread, leveraging the JVM's threading mechanisms.

Sending Email

Sending and receiving email in the JVM involves a low-level API called JavaMail.

JavaMail is a specification and implementation that maps a number of mail-related APIs very closely, without being prejudiced toward how those APIs are used. After all, many libraries that wrap services try to be opinionated about "proper usage" – thus, a database library might **force** programmers into using transactions.[1] Those opinions might be worthwhile and justified, but they're also limiting. JavaMail and other such libraries try to represent the underlying protocols as they actually are, rather than suggesting proper usage that may not be appropriate for all cases.

This isn't a *bad* thing, but it's not a *good* thing, either, because the email protocols are designed for *efficient* use and not *ease* of use. Writing code using JavaMail directly tends to make one appreciate good email clients that hide all of the underlying APIs from the user experience.

Spring makes *sending* email using the SMTP protocol very easy, using an interface called `JavaMailSender`. However, it doesn't really help us *read* emails without going to

---

[1] Being forced into using transactions probably isn't a bad idea for a database library.

© Felipe Gutierrez, Joseph B. Ottinger 2022
F. Gutierrez and J. B. Ottinger, *Introducing Spring Framework 6*, https://doi.org/10.1007/978-1-4842-8637-1_11

yet another Spring module, which is out of scope for this book;[2] we're going to get to use JavaMail to read messages.

Another issue working with email is that you need an email server, much like you need a database to work with JDBC. Spring happily embeds the H2 database for us if it's in the classpath, but email servers are a *bit* more complex to deploy than a simple embedded database.

We're going to leverage `https://mailtrap.io`, by Railsware, which provides SMTP, IMAP, and POP3 endpoints for testing emails.

Note   This is not meant to be an endorsement or recommendation of Railsware, but `mailtrap.io` is incredibly useful for what it's designed to do; the way we're using the site doesn't push it to its limits, and there may be costs to using `mailtrap` in certain ways. Be careful, even though we've found no issues using `mailtrap` in the process of developing this chapter. It is worth saying that `mailtrap.io` helped your authors avoid a ton of documentation and deployment work.

It's also worth noting that **this chapter is the first chapter whose tests are not working out of the box** in the sample source code. You're going to need to provide your own credentials for `mailtrap` – or whatever service you choose to use – and the sample source code does not have *our* credentials in it.

Before we can really start developing an email service, we need to set up a `mailtrap.io` account.

Set Up MailTrap

First, open up `https://mailtrap.io` in a web browser. In the upper right-hand corner, you'll see "Log In" and "Sign Up" buttons; go ahead and sign up. You can use an existing GMail, GitHub, or Office365 account, or you can sign up using your own individual email address if you like.

---

[2] The Spring Integration project has some convenient classes for reading email, but Spring Integration is really targeted at building execution pipelines. It's very powerful, and it's a common architecture, but event processing on that scale is a subject beyond what this chapter is targeting.

That will take you to an account page, where you will have a single inbox (called "My Inbox") by default. The SMTP settings tab is going to be important; there's a link to "Show Credentials" which will show you a set of SMTP and POP3 settings, which we'll need for this chapter.

On initialization, the page looks a lot like Figure 11-1.

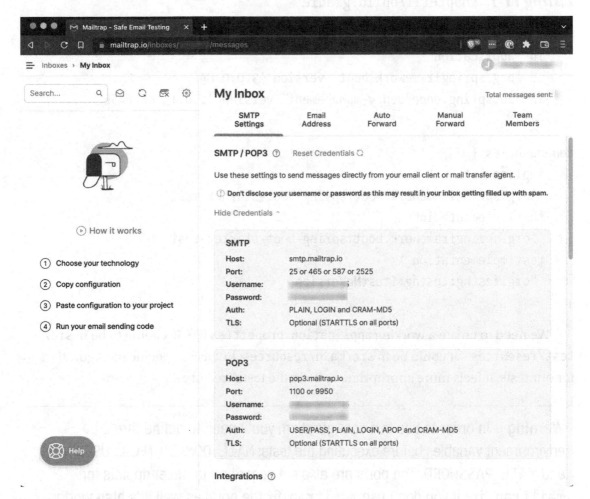

Figure 11-1. *MailTrap Displaying SMTP Configuration Settings*

We're going to use that configuration data to build an `application.properties` for our tests.

Before we can do that, though, we need to create our project.

The Email Aspect of the Project

The project descriptor itself is pretty simple. Note that we're including the `spring-boot-starter-test`, TestNG, and `spring-boot-starter-mail` dependencies.

Listing 11-1. `chapter11/build.gradle`

```
plugins {
    id "application"
    id 'org.springframework.boot' version '3.0.0-M4'
    id 'io.spring.dependency-management' version '1.0.13.RELEASE'
}

dependencies {
    implementation \
      'org.springframework.boot:spring-boot-starter-mail'
    testImplementation \
      'org.springframework.boot:spring-boot-starter-test'
    testImplementation \
      "org.testng:testng:$testNgVersion"
}
```

We need to create a working `application.properties` file. It's going to be in `src/test/resources` – it could be in `src/main/resources`, but as its specific configuration for our tests, it feels more appropriate to be in the test directory.

Warning   In order to use this configuration, you'll need to define three environment variables before executing the tests: `MAIL_DOMAIN`, `MAIL_USERNAME`, and `MAIL_PASSWORD`. The ports are also set according to the endpoints for `mailtrap.io`; if you don't use `mailtrap`, fix the ports as well. It's **also** worth noting that some of these configuration decisions were arbitrary; we really **should** define the ports in environment variables, but then you also have to consider that the POP3 server name might not follow the convention of `pop3.domain`, and at some point, it turns into turtles all the way down. Feel free to adjust the configuration as desired and such that it works for you.

Listing 11-2. `chapter11/src/test/resources/application.properties`

```
mail.domain=${MAIL_DOMAIN}

spring.mail.protocol=smtp
spring.mail.host=smtp.${MAIL_DOMAIN}
spring.mail.port=2525
spring.mail.username=${MAIL_USERNAME}
spring.mail.password=${MAIL_PASSWORD}
spring.mail.properties.mail.smtp.auth = true
spring.mail.properties.mail.smtp.starttls.enable = true
pop3.host=pop3.${MAIL_DOMAIN}
pop3.port=9950

mail.address=${spring.mail.username}@${MAIL_DOMAIN}
```

It's time for the fun part! Let's build an `EmailService`.

There are two main purposes for an email service: writing emails and reading them. It turns out that Spring makes **writing** emails – sending them – pretty trivial, because there's a `JavaMailSender` interface that's part of Spring; if we have our application properties set up correctly (as shown in Listing 11-2, assuming your environment variables are set properly), we can *trivially* send mail with `JavaMailSender`.

Reading email is a little different that writing email. When you *send* mail, you typically use a standardized protocol called SMTP,[3] although other custom protocols may exist.

When you *read* mail, you have many, many more options. One of the simplest protocols is called POP3,[4] although another common protocol is IMAP,[5] and there are *other* alternatives to these protocols, as well as variants of them. Each one has strengths and weaknesses; POP3 is simple, but quite easy to use, and IMAP is probably the most common and full-featured of the protocols, providing the concept of "folders" to emails while adding some complexity to the process of retrieving emails. (As it turns out, some of that complexity will affect how we use POP3, but it'll be rather mild.)

---

[3] SMTP stands for "Simple Mail Transfer Protocol," as described as of this writing by RFC 8314, which can be read from `https://datatracker.ietf.org/doc/html/rfc8314` – and "Simple Mail Transfer Protocol" is an apt description, thankfully.

[4] POP3 stands for "Post Office Protocol," version 3, and is described by RFC 1081 – and many others. See `https://datatracker.ietf.org/doc/html/rfc1081` for a starting point.

[5] IMAP is the "Internet Message Access Protocol" and is described by RFC 9051, at `https://datatracker.ietf.org/doc/html/rfc9051`.

For our purposes, we're going to stay simple and use POP3S – a secure version of POP3 – to read email. It turns out that JavaMail represents most of the protocols pretty cleanly at the API level, so we could migrate to another protocol without changing much code, but to keep our configuration and code simple, we're going to ignore flexibility and target *usefulness*.

There are other concerns, however, which we'll mention as soon as we take a look at our EmailService.

Listing 11-3. chapter11/src/main/java/md/EmailService.java

```java
package md;

import jakarta.mail.*;
import org.springframework.beans.factory.annotation.Value;
import org.springframework.mail.SimpleMailMessage;
import org.springframework.mail.javamail.JavaMailSender;
import org.springframework.stereotype.Service;

import java.util.ArrayList;
import java.util.Arrays;
import java.util.List;
import java.util.Properties;
import java.util.function.BiConsumer;
import java.util.function.Predicate;

@Service
public class EmailService {
  // attributes
  private final JavaMailSender sender;
  private final Properties sessionProperties;
  private final String username;
  private final String password;
  private final int pop3Port;
  private final String pop3Host;

  EmailService(JavaMailSender sender,
               @Value("${pop3.host}")
               String pop3Host,
```

```
        @Value("${pop3.port}")
        int pop3Port,
        @Value("${spring.mail.username}")
        String username,
        @Value("${spring.mail.password}")
        String password) {
  this.sender = sender;
  this.username = username;
  this.password = password;
  this.pop3Host = pop3Host;
  this.pop3Port = pop3Port;
  sessionProperties = new Properties();
  sessionProperties.put("mail.pop3.host", pop3Host);
}

/**
 * This method is responsible for sending an email
 * via the <code></code>JavaMailSender</code> reference.
 * It uses parameters implicitly used to construct the
 <code>sender</code>
 * via Spring's application configuration.
 */
public void send(
  String from,
  String to,
  String subject,
  String content
) {
  var message = new SimpleMailMessage();
  message.setFrom(from);
  message.setTo(to);
  message.setSubject(subject);
  message.setText(content);
  sender.send(message);
}
```

171

```java
/*
 * All of these methods are used to <i>read</i> emails.
 */
private SimpleMailMessage cloneMessage(Message m) {
  try {
    var msg = new SimpleMailMessage();
    msg.setFrom(m.getFrom()[0].toString());
    msg.setTo(m.getAllRecipients()[0].toString());
    msg.setSubject(m.getSubject());
    msg.setText(m.getContent().toString());

    return msg;
  } catch (Exception e) {
    throw new RuntimeException(e);
  }
}

private Session getSession() {
  var emailSession = Session.getDefaultInstance(sessionProperties);
  return emailSession;
}

private Store getStore(Session session) throws MessagingException {
  var emailStore = session.getStore(
    new URLName("pop3",
      pop3Host,
      pop3Port,
      null,
      username,
      password
    ));
  emailStore.connect();
  return emailStore;
}

private Folder getFolder(Store store) throws MessagingException {
  var emailFolder = store.getFolder("INBOX");
  emailFolder.open(Folder.READ_WRITE);
```

```java
    return emailFolder;
}

public void processMessages(
    Predicate<Message> predicate,
    BiConsumer<Folder, Message> consumer) {
    var session = getSession();
    try (var store = getStore(session)) {
        try (var folder = getFolder(store)) {
            var messages = folder.getMessages();
            Arrays
                .stream(messages)
                .filter(predicate)
                .forEach(m -> consumer.accept(folder, m));
        }
    } catch (MessagingException e) {
        throw new RuntimeException(e);
    }
}

public List<SimpleMailMessage> getMessages() {
    var messages = new ArrayList<SimpleMailMessage>();
    processMessages(
        message -> true,
        (folder, message) -> {
            SimpleMailMessage m = cloneMessage(message);
            messages.add(m);
        });
    return messages;
}

public void deleteMessage(Folder folder, Message message) {
    try {
        var flags = new Flags(Flags.Flag.DELETED);
        folder.setFlags(new Message[]{message}, flags, true);
```

```
    } catch (MessagingException e) {
      throw new RuntimeException(e);
    }
  }
}
```

There's a *lot* to unpack here, as it's one of the longest classes we've seen so far in the entire book. Let's walk through each block.

Our first block of *code* is pretty straightforward, consisting of a set of attributes and the class constructor. The JavaMailSender is, as stated, a Spring interface that provides access to the JavaMail Session class, itself designed to handle sending *and* receiving email, but JavaMailSender doesn't really expose everything we need to read email – it only exposes methods like createMimeMessage() and variants of a send() method.

The other attributes of our constructor are populated values from our application. properties and will be used to get access to a POP3 inbox to read emails. We also save off a Properties object, again to provide easy access to a POP3 email session.

The send() method in EmailService is very straightforward. It's meant to send simple text only; to send HTML, you'd use sender to create a MIME message and populate it accordingly. Instead, we're using a SimpleMailMessage.[6] Most of building a multipart MIME message is fairly straightforward, but it's out of scope for this text. The EmailService.send() doesn't do any template rendering, although nothing would prevent a user from creating text using Thymeleaf or any other template library and using the output from *that* library as input for send().

After that, we get to more complex mechanisms. To understand what's going on, we need to consider how JavaMail reads emails.

To read emails in JavaMail, you access a number of resources, much like one accesses JDBC.[7]

---

[6] A SimpleMailMessage is an object representing an email that has a very straightforward representation of email – from, to, cc, bcc, and subject – and body contents are represented, without having to get into multipart messages with downloadable content. See https://docs.spring.io/spring-framework/docs/current/javadoc-api/org/springframework/mail/SimpleMailMessage.html for more.

[7] Remember, in JDBC, you get a Connection, and then you use that to get a PreparedStatement, from which you get a ResultSet, as the typical happy path for user code.

1. First, we get a Session.

2. Then, we get a Store from the Session, using an internal URL for the store type ("POP3" in this case). A Store, in email contexts, is "where emails are stored."

3. We get a named Folder from the store.

4. At last, we can access Message entities from the Folder, which are populated on demand, much as JDBC query results are accessed through an active Connection – if the resources like the Folder are closed, we lose access to the message attributes unless we've already copied them off.

We know, given the nature of JavaMail data access, that we'll need to have a way to "save off" email contents; our first "access" method is cloneMessage, which gives us a SimpleMailMessage based on the contents of a Message. We're not going for accuracy here, only sufficiency, as we're not replicating JavaMail in this chapter; thus, we copy off only the first from header, the first to header, and the subject and simple text contents. This method is insufficient for any complex email addresses.

After that, we have a number of cascading methods:

1. The getSession() method returns a JavaMail Session.

2. The getStore(Session) method takes a Session and returns a POP3-based Store, based on the properties used to create the EmailService.

3. The getFolder(Store) method gets a named Folder (INBOX) from a Store and makes sure we can write to it for convenience' sake.

Our next method is called processMessages() and it's ... interesting. It takes two arguments: a Predicate<Message> and a BiConsumer<Folder, Message>.

What processMessages() is designed to do is to read every message in the INBOX folder and select every message that matches the predicate; for every message that matches the predicate, apply the consumer.

Warning   Our EmailService has a getMessages() method, but processMessages() uses getMessages() from the Folder and not the EmailService. We do not have a cyclic dependency, we promise.

We use this in getMessages(), the very next method in EmailService. This method builds a local List<SimpleMailMessage> and then passes in a predicate that always returns true – thus, it matches every message – and a consumer that adds a cloned message (using cloneMessage(), naturally) to the internal getMessages() List and then returns that list.

We'll see more of how we can apply processMessages() when we see our test class, but first we have one last utility method, deleteMessage() – which takes a Folder and a Message, making it a candidate for the consumer in processMessages(). (It doesn't use processMessages() to do anything because it's working on a reference we should already have, that we presumably got from getMessages() or something like it.) That will, in fact, be exactly how the method is used in our test class.

In fact, it's time to *see* our test class so we can tie all of this together and verify it works.

Warning   Remember, none of this *will* work until you've set the runtime properties correctly. How to set environment variables depends heavily on what operating system you use and how you invoke the test.

This class contains a reference to the EmailService, a "sending email address" in source, a "generated title" in title (generated from a UUID), and contains a utility method to send email. The sendEmail method returns a long, which is a simple "clock time" in milliseconds it takes to run the method to send email; we don't *need* that but it will be useful in the second half of this chapter.

Now let's take a look at an actual test class for EmailService.

Before we get to the test, we need a configuration. It's really just a placeholder for the Spring configuration annotations; in a "real application," we'd use @ SpringBootApplication and get everything this class has automatically, except for @ EnableScheduling, which will show up in the next section of this chapter. We could have more than one configuration (one with @EnableScheduling, one without) but there's not a benefit in doing so; all @EnableScheduling does is tell Spring that it needs to instantiate the scheduling service and scan for scheduling events, which we'll cover soon.

Listing 11-4. chapter11/src/test/java/md/TestConfiguration.java

```
package md;

import org.springframework.boot.autoconfigure.EnableAutoConfiguration;
import org.springframework.context.annotation.ComponentScan;
import org.springframework.context.annotation.Configuration;
import org.springframework.scheduling.annotation.EnableScheduling;

@Configuration
@EnableAutoConfiguration
@ComponentScan
@EnableScheduling
public class TestConfiguration {
}
```

Now we get to our actual email service test.

Listing 11-5. chapter11/src/test/java/md/TestEmailService.java

```
package md;

import jakarta.mail.MessagingException;
import org.springframework.beans.factory.annotation.Autowired;
import org.springframework.beans.factory.annotation.Value;
import org.springframework.boot.test.context.SpringBootTest;
import org.springframework.test.context.testng.AbstractTestNGSpringContextTests;
import org.testng.annotations.Test;

import java.time.LocalDate;
import java.util.UUID;
import java.util.concurrent.atomic.AtomicBoolean;

import static org.testng.Assert.assertTrue;

@SpringBootTest(classes = TestConfiguration.class)
public class TestEmailService extends AbstractTestNGSpringContextTests {
    @Autowired
```

```java
EmailService mailService;
@Value("${mail.address}")
String source;
String title = UUID.randomUUID().toString();

@Test
void testSendEmail() {
  mailService.send(
    source,
    source,
    title,
    "This is a sample email, sent at " + LocalDate.now()
  );
}

@Test(dependsOnMethods = "testSendEmail")
void checkReceiveEmailFromInbox() {
  var messages = mailService.getMessages();
  boolean found = false;
  for (var message : messages) {
    if (title.equals(message.getSubject())) {
      found = true;
    }
  }
  assertTrue(found, "failed to find message with matching title");
}

@Test(dependsOnMethods = "testSendEmail")
void checkReceivedEmailByTitle() {
  var found = new AtomicBoolean(false);
  mailService.processMessages(message -> {
      try {
        return message.getSubject().equals(title);
      } catch (MessagingException e) {
        throw new RuntimeException(e);
      }
    },
```

```
  (folder, message) -> {
    mailService.deleteMessage(folder, message);
    found.set(true);

  });
  assertTrue(found.get(), "failed to find message with matching title");
 }
}
```

The first thing we notice about this test is that the @SpringBootTest has a reference to TestConfiguration.class so the test has a configuration.

We also have references to a "sending email address" in source, and a "generated title" in title (generated from a UUID), and contains a utility method to send email. (We don't need a reference to body content as we're not leveraging it for the tests.)

Our first test is testSendEmail(), which is quite simple: it simply calls the EmailService.send() method. An error here means that the send itself fails (an exception will be propagated, after all); we're not testing to verify that the email was sent yet. That's the *next* test, checkReceiveEmailFromInbox().

The checkReceiveEmailFromInbox() test depends on the success of testSendEmail() – after all, if we can't send email, we don't want to search for the email that wasn't able to be sent!

This method uses the EmailService.processMessages() method; the predicate looks for any message whose subject matches the value of the title string (the random UUID, generated for this test). The consumer simply informs the test that yes, the title was found. The test then checks to make sure that the found value is set to true – meaning that the predicate managed to find an email with a matching title.

Note   We are using an AtomicBoolean because lambdas in Java require either final or *effectively* final references; the use of AtomicBoolean means we don't have to declare a final array of booleans with one element in it, like final boolean found[1];.

We have one more test, which is very similar to the checkReceiveEmailFromInbox() method and, in fact, was initially copied from it. The checkReceivedEmailByTitle() method uses a predicate that only returns messages that match a given title, and it calls mailService.deleteMessage() with the Folder and Message when it matches a message. As a result, if it finds a *matching message* (i.e., the title is what we expect), we not only mark the message as being *found*, but we delete it so we can run the test without filling the POP3 mailbox with junk.

So what we have, then, is a utility class (`EmailService`) which is able to use Spring's `JavaMailSender` to send email trivially, assuming that our configuration is correct, and we've also built some utility methods in `EmailService` that demonstrate how we can also use `JavaMail` directly to *read* email.

`EmailService`, as we've written it, is probably not inherently broadly useful; it sends only plain text email, and its mechanism for reading emails is locked into POP3 instead of the more powerful IMAP protocol (for simplicity's sake), and the way that it reads mail is to literally iterate through an entire mail folder. With that said, it's not much of a leap from what is a very simple class usable only for demonstration purposes to something that might be useful in production code, especially after we look at the asynchronous capabilities in Spring.

Asynchronous Tasks in Spring

Spring has multiple approaches to handling asynchronous invocation of tasks. Chapter 10 already demonstrated the *architectural* mechanism of using message brokers through JMS (and similar possibilities exist for other protocols like MQTT or even specific brokers like RabbitMQ). However, the JVM itself is also multithreaded, and Spring helps us leverage that for asynchronous invocation as well.

There are, *generally speaking*, three ways you can leverage multithreaded invocation.

1. You can manage it manually, just as you would *without* Spring, by creating an `ExecutorService` reference and managing dispatch through it.

2. You can use Spring's `@Async` annotation to mark a method as supporting asynchronous invocation through a configuration.

3. You can use a Spring scheduler to dispatch method calls based on local clock time or at regular intervals.

Doing asynchronous invocation without Spring isn't very useful in a book *covering* Spring, and it's very well covered by the Java tutorial and Java documentation, anyway. We're going to ignore that possibility (although it's worth noting that Spring has ways to help you create an `ExecutorService` for its own asynchronous dispatch, it's not difficult, but it's also not particularly instructive.)

The `@Async` annotation is fascinating, but not incredibly useful for most applications. If the method being annotated with `@Async` returns nothing (as a method returning `void`), `@Async` invokes it in a separate (configurable) `ExecutorService` thread and returns immediately while the invoked method is run by the `ExecutorService` thread. If the method returns a `Future<V>` with data in it, it will *also* be invoked in the executor service, but it has to have been designed to work with asynchronous invocation.

It's not particularly difficult to work with – instead of returning, say, a `List<String>`, an asynchronous method would return `Future<List<String>>`.

The only *problem* with that – perhaps a better way to write this is as a "problem," with quotes – is that the use of the `@Async` annotation necessitates a change in how we write the underlying method in the first place. We can't just say "Oh, this method is meant to be invoked asynchronously" and be done; we have to use a specific return type (the `Future<V>`) at the very least.

As a result, methods marked as `@Async` are curiosities, effectively; you're just as well off building your own `Callable<V>` instances and invoking them as asynchronous methods explicitly, since that's simpler (being part of the language and library specifications already), and adding `@Async` does very little other than offering (potentially) a bridge to Spring configuring an `ExecutorService` for you, implicitly.

The third method[8] is to use an actual scheduler to run tasks at specific times or at fixed rates. Let's dig into this, since it's a little more generally useful than `@Async` would be.

Note   This is not to imply that @Async is useless! It's certainly got its own application; the fact that it uses a Spring-configured thread pool has its own power. It's just that for *most* users, @Async is going to be of limited utility compared to other options.

---

[8] You didn't lose track of the fact that we're iterating through a list of options for asynchronous invocation, did you?

Adding Scheduling Events in Spring

For asynchronous scheduling, we're going to create a "SystemMonitor" service that indicates whether a "system" is working or not. It will start as an interface, and we'll create two implementations that change the monitor's "working" state over time to validate the scheduling mechanism.

Here's the interface itself:

Listing 11-6. `chapter11/src/main/java/md/SystemMonitor.java`

```java
package md;

public interface SystemMonitor {
  default boolean isWorking() {
    return true;
  }

  default void start() {
  }
}
```

We have a `start()` method so we can potentially control when to begin the state can change; by default, the interface does nothing worthwhile.

There are a few options we have for scheduled events.

1. We have a *fixed-rate* system; events are triggered every so often, regardless of how long the events take to process. If an event takes longer than the elapsed time, new events will be scheduled and event overlap may occur.

2. We have an *elapsed-rate* system, where event scheduling occurs after an event is **finished** – if the period is 1 second and event takes 5 seconds to process, the next event will be scheduled for 1 second after the processing is completed.

3. We have a specific time system, based on `cron`, where we can specify that events are triggered based on time and date patterns; we can specify that events are triggered on the first second of the fifth minute of the seventh hour of every Monday in a given month, for example.

First, we'll look at the fixed-rate option.

Let's implement a timed service that – once started – has an internal countdown until the monitor "stops working."

Note   In practice, we would have a method in the monitor services to do *something* when the indicator starts to fail. We might send a warning email to someone in operations, for example, or attempt to restart the failing services. As this is only an example, we just record the state and move on.

Here's a "SystemMonitor" that runs the countdown at a fixed rate:

Listing 11-7. chapter11/src/test/java/md/FixedRateMonitorService.java

```java
package md;

import org.slf4j.Logger;
import org.slf4j.LoggerFactory;
import org.springframework.scheduling.annotation.Scheduled;
import org.springframework.stereotype.Service;

@Service
public class FixedRateMonitorService implements SystemMonitor {
  boolean started = false;
  int countdown = 3;
  Logger logger = LoggerFactory.getLogger(this.getClass());

  @Override
  public void start() {
    started = true;
  }

  @Override
  public boolean isWorking() {
    // it's "working" as long as the tripwire time
    // has not elapsed
    return countdown > 0;
  }
```

```
@Scheduled(fixedRate = 1000)
void updateWorkingState() {
  if (started) {
    countdown = Math.max(countdown - 1, 0);

    logger.info(
      String.format(
        "Monitor service countdown: %d, status: %b",
        countdown,
        isWorking()));
  }
 }
}
```

The class is marked as a @Service so Spring will pick it up. It has some working variables to keep track of whether it's been started or not, as well as a countdown, and a Logger reference so we can cleanly output the countdown events as they're issued.

The start() method is just a flag to indicate whether the countdown should run or not; our test code can use this to begin the countdown, and the isWorking() method simply indicates whether the countdown has finished or not.

Then we hit the interesting bit: the updateWorkingState() method.

First, note the @Scheduled annotation, which has a fixedRate value of 1000. This means that the method will be invoked every 1000 milliseconds – roughly every second, basically.[9] In the method itself, *if* the start() method has been called, we decrement the countdown with a minimum value of 0 (just in case the service keeps being in "started" state after it's been started!) and issue a log message that includes the new values.

Let's see a test that validates whether the FixedRateMonitorService works or not.

---

[9] The timing of scheduled events is not guaranteed. If we specify 1000 milliseconds, it'll generally be very close to 1000 milliseconds, but this is not a real-time scheduler, so you may see variations of a few milliseconds here and there.

Listing 11-8. chapter11/src/test/java/md/TestFixedRateService.java

```java
package md;

import org.springframework.beans.factory.annotation.Autowired;
import org.springframework.boot.test.context.SpringBootTest;
import org.springframework.test.context.testng.AbstractTestNG
SpringContextTests;
import org.testng.annotations.Test;

import static org.testng.Assert.*;

@SpringBootTest(classes = TestConfiguration.class)
public class TestFixedRateService extends
AbstractTestNGSpringContextTests {
  @Autowired
  FixedRateMonitorService fixedRate;

  @Test
  void fixedRateTest() throws InterruptedException {
    fixedRate.start();
    // fixed rate iterates every second
    Thread.sleep(4000L);
    assertFalse(fixedRate.isWorking());
  }
}
```

This is a fairly simple test. We include the TestConfiguration for our configuration, of course, and get a reference to the FixedRateMonitorService by type; we could have used a qualifier as well.

The fixedRateTest() starts the scheduler countdown (with fixedRate.start()) and then waits 4 seconds, because we know the FixedRateMonitorService should be able to countdown entirely in 3 seconds as a worst case.

After the time has elapsed, we can validate the monitoring service' state: if it's still working after 4 seconds, the timer has *not* run and we have a failure condition; our scheduling hasn't worked as expected.

Let's take a look at one of our other scheduling options, the `cron`-based option.

The UNIX `cron` utility allows us to specify when something can happen based on a specially formatted string, with six fields separated by spaces. The six fields are as follows:

Second	This is a number from 0 to 59.
Minute	This is a number from 0 to 59.
Hour	This is a number from 0 to 23.
day of the month	This is a number from 1 to 31.
Month	This is a number, from 1 to 12, or a three-letter abbreviation for the month from the Gregorian calendar, so "1" is equivalent to "JAN," which means that the scheduling event matches "January."
day of the week	This is a number, from 0 to 7, with 0 *and* 7 meaning "Sunday" or a three-letter abbreviation matching the day as well, so Sunday can *also* be expressed as "SUN."

If the field isn't significant for us, we can use an asterisk (*) for numeric fields, and the day-of-week and day-of-month fields can also use a question mark as a wildcard. (They mean the same thing for nonnumeric fields.)

You can also specify intervals and multiple values, so it's relatively easy to say "every 10 seconds" by using something like */10 for the second field, or you can say that an event must run on the 7th and 21st of every month by using 7,21 for the day-of-month field. If you'd like to read more about this (as well as get a more complete reference), see "Improved Cron Expressions"[10] for an excellent summary of the feature from when it was introduced.

Thus, if we wanted to schedule an event for January 7, at 6:03 p.m., at the 30th second, we could do so with the following expressions:

```
30 3 18 7 JAN ? 30 3 18 7 1 *
```

---

[10] See https://spring.io/blog/2020/11/10/new-in-spring-5-3-improved-cron-expressions.

This breaks down like this:

30	The first field is the second to execute, so we're saying "at the 30th second" of a minute.
3	This is the minute field, so it's the third minute of an hour.
18	This is the sixth hour after noon, thus "18" using military time conventions; combined with the minute and second fields, we have "6:03:30 p.m."
7	This is the day of a given month, thus "the seventh day."
JAN or 1	As January is the first month of the Gregorian calendar, and its "short form" is "JAN," both of these values are equivalent; combined with the date of the month, we now have suggested that the cron expression matches only January 7th of any given year.
? and *	These are both acceptable wildcards for the day of the week; as we've specified a specific date, we use a wildcard here to specify that we don't care what day of the week that date falls on.

If we wanted to trigger an event at 1:00 a.m. every Monday, we could use the following equivalent expressions:

```
0 0 1 * * MON 0 0 1 * * 1
```

So let's take a look at a `CrontabMonitorService`, which will functionally be the same as our `FixedRateMonitorService` except with different scheduling.

Instead of every second, we'll trigger the event at the start of every *minute* (so our cron expression won't be simply a set of wildcards.)

Listing 11-9. chapter11/src/test/java/md/CrontabMonitorService.java

```java
package md;

import org.slf4j.Logger;
import org.slf4j.LoggerFactory;
import org.springframework.scheduling.annotation.Scheduled;
import org.springframework.stereotype.Service;
@Service

public class CrontabMonitorService implements SystemMonitor {
  boolean started=false;
  boolean valid=true;
```

```java
Logger logger = LoggerFactory.getLogger(this.getClass());

@Scheduled(cron="0 * * * * *")
void updateWorkingState() {
  if(started) {
    valid=false;
  }
  logger.info(
    String.format(
      "Monitor service status: %b",
      isWorking()));
}

@Override
public void start() {
  started=true;
}

@Override
public boolean isWorking() {
  // it's "working" as long as the tripwire time
  // has not elapsed
  return valid;
}
}
```

We can't have a service without testing it, of course, so let's create a test. The test is a little more fun to read, because it needs to anticipate when the monitoring service **should** fail – so most of the code in our test is actually dedicated to calculating a delay that waits until the *second* second of the *next* minute.

Thus, if you start this test at the 59th second of a given clock minute, it will finish the test in roughly three seconds (because of the countdown timer), whereas if you start it just as a clock minute begins, you might get to wait for a full minute before it finishes.

Listing 11-10. chapter11/src/test/java/md/TestCrontabService.java

```java
package md;

import org.springframework.beans.factory.annotation.Autowired;
import org.springframework.boot.test.context.SpringBootTest;
import
org.springframework.test.context.testng.AbstractTestNGSpringContextTests;
import org.testng.annotations.Test;

import java.time.Instant;
import java.time.temporal.ChronoUnit;

import static org.testng.Assert.*;

@SpringBootTest(classes = TestConfiguration.class)
public class TestCrontabService extends AbstractTestNGSpringContextTests {
  @Autowired
  CrontabMonitorService crontab;

  @Test
  void crontabTest() throws InterruptedException {
    assertNotNull(crontab);
    var delay = Instant
      .now()
      .truncatedTo(ChronoUnit.MINUTES)
      .plus(1, ChronoUnit.MINUTES)
      .plus(2, ChronoUnit.SECONDS)
      .minusMillis(System.currentTimeMillis())
      .toEpochMilli();
    crontab.start();
    assertTrue(crontab.isWorking());
    Thread.sleep(delay);
    assertFalse(crontab.isWorking());
  }
}
```

Summary

This chapter has gone over a few different topics: the first was email, with `JavaMailSender` being used to *send* mail via Spring; we also saw how to *read* email using the JavaMail API directly.

After that, we explored the scheduling services in Spring, which – combined with the mail sender – could, for example, send out regularly scheduled emails from an application at need.

In our next chapter, we're going to explore using dynamic languages to provide functionality to a Spring application.

PART IV

The New Spring I/O

CHAPTER 12

Using Dynamic Languages

In Chapter 11, we saw how we can send email using Spring's built-in mail sending classes. In this chapter, we're going to look into another corner altogether, the ability of Spring to leverage actual scripting languages directly as Spring components.

We're going to mostly look at Groovy, but Beanshell and JRuby support is also included; they're just less likely to fit well into most developers' paradigms.

It's also worth pointing out that scripts, in this context, refer to *actual scripts* and not compiled versions of languages that *can be scripted*. Groovy, for example, can be compiled to Java bytecode, or it can be run as a literal script.

If you're compiling to Java bytecode, then there's nothing special to be done; you can annotate the classes with @Component or @Service (or whatever stereotype is important) and let Spring load the classes from the classpath, just as if you were using Java. We saw this all the way back in Chapter 1, in fact, with Kotlin.

With that said, though, we can leverage JSR 223[1] to interpret various language sources from various *places*.

---

[1] JSR-223 is "Scripting for the Java Platform" and can be found at www.jcp.org/en/jsr/detail?id=223; it covers the specification for a generalized scripting engine and is often used to load JavaScript or Groovy into the Java runtime.

© Felipe Gutierrez, Joseph B. Ottinger 2022
F. Gutierrez and J. B. Ottinger, *Introducing Spring Framework 6*, https://doi.org/10.1007/978-1-4842-8637-1_12

Loading Functionality Dynamically with Groovy

Our `build.gradle` files have all been written in a language called "Groovy,"[2] originally designed as a dynamic language for the JVM and roughly analogous in a lot of ways to Ruby. Like Kotlin, it's semantically very similar to Java, with a more sparse grammar than Java.

That may or may not be a good thing; in the end, Groovy remains quite viable but is less popular than Kotlin according to the TIOBE index.[3]

What we're going to do is simple: we're going to build a `MessageService` interface that defines a simple `getMessage()` accessor, very much like our "Hello World" functionality from Chapter 1. Then we're going to implement it in three different ways, all with Groovy creating our Spring beans.

There are some limitations to such components implemented in dynamic languages.

When we're using precompiled code, we can specify values to be provided to beans through their constructors. When we're using dynamic languages, we can specify *properties* but not *constructor arguments*.

We're also somewhat limited to using XML for our configuration. The Java configuration for dynamic scripts would, after all, just use the JSR-223 `ScriptEngine` to load classes and coerce types into something the JVM can use, which would involve a decent amount of boilerplate code. It's doable, but not really instructive; if you want the dynamic resolution, you can isolate part of your configuration into an XML file (as we've done for this chapter) and mix the XML configuration in with your Java configuration and get the best of both worlds.

With all that said, let's dive in. First, as always, we want to take a look at our build file. This is very much a simple build configuration, with the only difference between it and most of our configurations is the inclusion of Groovy.

Listing 12-1. `chapter12/build.gradle`

```
dependencies {
    implementation \
    "org.springframework:spring-core:$springFrameworkVersion"
```

---

[2] Groovy's website is `https://groovy-lang.org/`.

[3] The TIOBE index is a rough indicator of programming language popularity, found at `www.tiobe.com/tiobe-index/` – as of this writing, Kotlin is at #29, Groovy is at #39, and Java itself sits strong at #3.

```
implementation \
"org.springframework:spring-context:$springFrameworkVersion"
implementation \
"org.springframework:spring-test:$springFrameworkVersion"
implementation \
"org.codehaus.groovy:groovy-all:3.0.12"
}
```

Next, we need to define our MessageService interface. It's going to be very simple:

Listing 12-2. chapter12/src/main/java/md/MessageService.java

```java
package md;

public interface MessageService {
  String getMessage();
}
```

Now things get a little more interesting.

The way you configure beans written with a dynamic language is to use a bean definition directive in XML. There are three predefined directives for dynamic languages:

1. <lang:groovy /> for dynamic beans written in Groovy

2. <lang:bsh /> for dynamic beans written in BeanShell, another scripting language targeting the JVM

3. <lang:std /> for dynamic beans written for *any* ScriptingEngine, where users specify which scripting engine is to be used

Most users will probably zero in on the Groovy mechanism, as it's the simplest and most straightforward, but advanced users might find themselves using <lang:std /> at some point.

When we specify a bean using <lang:groovy />, we can specify that the script is to be loaded from the classpath or filesystem, using the script-source attribute. If we don't use script-source, we can provide the script content in the configuration file itself, using <lang:inline-script/>.

We can also specify a refresh-check-delay attribute, which specifies a time period in milliseconds after which the dynamic bean's content will be refreshed. This means that if you're loading from the filesystem (as opposed to loading from a java archive, a zip file, or some other static resource), you can edit the file during runtime and see changes reflected live in your running application.

Note   We're not demonstrating refresh-check-delay in this chapter, because reflecting live filesystem changes is essentially difficult to do in a book, but this is probably the *absolute best feature* of the dynamic scripting facility in Spring, because it allows you to do live development of features in a running container, without relying on special "development" modes that do live reloading, etc. What's more, since the dynamic languages tend to be a bit more forgiving than Java itself is, it's fantastic for rapid prototyping. For this feature, you would add a filesystem location to the classpath and load the scripts from the filesystem; change the script, with refresh-check-delay set, and your script will be executed as it is at any given moment, including your live edits.

With all that said, let's keep going further.

The Simplest Dynamic MessageService

First, let's take a look at a very simple implementation of our MessageService interface in Groovy, just to get a sense of what's required and what the code might look like.

Listing 12-3. chapter12/src/test/resources/scripts/gmessage.groovy

```groovy
import md.MessageService

class GMessage implements MessageService {
    @Override
    String getMessage() {
        return 'hello world, man'
    }
}
```

Everything here maps directly to what we'd expect in Java, with the exception of a `package` declaration and some of the standard Java grammar such as the line-terminating semicolons. The semicolons are unnecessary in Groovy, of course, and the package isn't exceptionally important here either; we can use one, but the scripts run in their own scripting context, so generally it's unnecessary.

The simplicity here is okay, because we're not trying to demonstrate how powerful Groovy can be – a simple implementation is enough, and we'll get to slightly more Groovy-ish scripts soon.

With this, now we're ready to see how it might be defined in a Spring configuration. Here's the first of three Spring configurations we'll see in this chapter; it simply loads our `gmessage.groovy` script from the classpath and provides it to our Spring application.

Listing 12-4. `chapter12/src/test/resources/simple-context.xml`

```xml
<?xml version="1.0" encoding="UTF-8"?>
<beans xmlns="http://www.springframework.org/schema/beans"
       xmlns:xsi="http://www.w3.org/2001/XMLSchema-instance"
       xmlns:lang="http://www.springframework.org/schema/lang"
       xsi:schemaLocation="http://www.springframework.org/schema/beans
       http://www.springframework.org/schema/beans/spring-beans.xsd
       http://www.springframework.org/schema/lang
       http://www.springframework.org/schema/lang/spring-lang.xsd">

    <lang:groovy name="gmessage"
        script-source="classpath:/scripts/gmessage.groovy"/>

</beans>
```

One thing to note here is that we've named our script (as `"gmessage"`) – but this isn't actually a Spring bean the way we normally think of it. If we were to get the bean names with `context.getBeanDefinitionNames()`, we would see a name like `org.springframework.scripting.groovy.GroovyScriptFactory#0` but not `gmessage`. Spring's `ApplicationContext` will, however, provide a bean reference if we use the name – i.e., `context.getBean("gmessage")` – or the type, like `context.getBean(MessageService.class)`.

That's pretty much it, but we haven't *used* it yet. Let's fix that.

First, we're going to define a base test class that provides basic functionality; it'll autowire a `MessageService` and give a hook for tests to specify what the `message` should be (as we're going to change the message for each of our examples). It will then check that the data it receives from the dynamic implementation matches what is expected. Remember, this is a *base* test class – we will extend it to provide actual testing functionality.

Listing 12-5. `chapter12/src/test/java/md/BaseMessageTest.java`

```java
package md;

import org.springframework.beans.factory.annotation.Autowired;
import org.springframework.context.ApplicationContext;
import
org.springframework.test.context.testng.AbstractTestNGSpringContextTests;
import org.testng.annotations.Test;

import static org.testng.Assert.assertEquals;

public abstract class BaseMessageTest extends
AbstractTestNGSpringContextTests {
  @Autowired
  MessageService messageService;
  @Autowired
  ApplicationContext context;

  public String getExpectedMessage() {
    return context.getBean("message", String.class);
  }

  @Test
  void testMessageService() {
    assertEquals(
      messageService.getMessage(),
      getExpectedMessage());
  }
}
```

Now we can look at an actual test, TestSimpleMessage.java:

Listing 12-6. chapter12/src/test/java/md/TestSimpleMessage.java

```java
package md;

import org.springframework.test.context.ContextConfiguration;
import org.testng.annotations.Test;

@ContextConfiguration(value = "classpath:/simple-context.xml")
@Test
public class TestSimpleMessage extends BaseMessageTest {
  @Override
  public String getExpectedMessage() {
    return "hello world, man";
  }
}
```

There's not a lot to this class: it exists to provide a place for the
@ContextConfiguration (to specify which context file to load), it includes the @Test
annotation to force TestNG to evaluate it as a test (as it has no tests of its own), and it has
an implementation of getExpectedMessage() that returns the message we expect, as a
constant. Running this test will execute the test from BaseMessageTest and validate that
the gmessage.groovy script does indeed return a message of "hello world, man" in
proper Groovy-speak.[4]

So what have we seen here? Not a lot – except that we're loading the gmessage.
groovy dynamically, at runtime. It's got constant behavior, so we're not really doing a lot
besides loading it; that's enough, but we can do more.

---

[4] I've been resisting the urge to use a lot of speech patterns and words from the 1970s this whole
chapter, and this is the only failure of which I am aware. I also wanted to wear bell-bottoms as I
wrote the chapter, but my wife says I don't have any. She burned them.

Using Spring to Configure the Dynamic MessageService

Let's try to configure our Spring bean loaded via script. First, let's take a look at a cgmessage.groovy – for "configurable groovy message."

Listing 12-7. `chapter12/src/test/resources/scripts/cgmessage.groovy`

```groovy
import md.MessageService

// we don't need a getMessage() because it's a groovy accessor
// by default.
class cgmessage implements MessageService {
    String message
}
```

This one-liner is roughly equivalent to a Java class that looks something like this, except with a few more boilerplate methods:

```java
import md.MessageService;

class cgmessage implements MessageService {
  String message;
  public void setMessage(String message) {
    this.message=message;
  }
  public String getMessage() {
    return message;
  }
}
```

We're also able to load the cgmessage dynamically, of course, which would be pretty handy if it did more for us. Configuring it looks just like one would expect a bean configuration to look like:

Listing 12-8. `chapter12/src/test/resources/property-context.xml`

```xml
<?xml version="1.0" encoding="UTF-8"?>
<beans xmlns="http://www.springframework.org/schema/beans"
       xmlns:xsi="http://www.w3.org/2001/XMLSchema-instance"
       xmlns:lang="http://www.springframework.org/schema/lang"
```

```
      xsi:schemaLocation="http://www.springframework.org/schema/beans
      http://www.springframework.org/schema/beans/spring-beans.xsd
      http://www.springframework.org/schema/lang
      http://www.springframework.org/schema/lang/spring-lang.xsd">

  <lang:groovy name="c.g.message"
              script-source="classpath:/scripts/cgmessage.groovy">
    <lang:property name="message" ref="message"/>
  </lang:groovy>

  <bean name="message" class="java.lang.String">
    <constructor-arg value="hi there" />
  </bean>
</beans>
```

As with our previous example, the only difference here is the use of the
`<lang:groovy/>` tag to declare that we're dynamically loading it and the `<lang:property />`
to configure it – note how we inject a reference to `message` (with `ref`) just like we would
with any other Spring configuration. We could have used `value` just as easily. The only
real limitation that such scripted beans have is that we can't use constructor arguments.

Of course, we can show you a configuration and a dynamic implementation, but
that's not worth a lot without a test to validate it. Instead of using constants for the
expected message value, let's load it from our Spring configuration.

Listing 12-9. `chapter12/src/test/java/md/TestPropertyMessage.java`

```
package md;

import org.springframework.test.context.ContextConfiguration;
import org.testng.annotations.Test;

@ContextConfiguration(value = "classpath:/property-context.xml")
@Test
public class TestPropertyMessage extends BaseMessageTest {
}
```

We're relying on the implementation of `BaseMessageTest` to do all of the work;
the main aspect of this test that differentiates it from any other of our tests is the
configuration filename.

Note   We could have used a test like Listing 3-17, where we have a list of configuration files in a `DataProvider`, loading each in a row and executing them in a series. However, Listing 3-17 was done mostly to show how that **could** be done; while there's value in doing so in a "real project," here we'd want to build up our list of configuration files, much as we did in Chapter 3, and work through what they do as we see them. The aggregate test adds no value.

Inline Dynamic Content

Let's see one more example. In Listing 12-8, we see a configuration that loads an external file from the classpath and sets a property in it; we don't *have* to use an external file at all. We can write our service implementation directly in our configuration.

Listing 12-10. `chapter12/src/test/resources/inline-context.xml`

```xml
<?xml version="1.0" encoding="UTF-8"?>
<beans xmlns="http://www.springframework.org/schema/beans"
       xmlns:xsi="http://www.w3.org/2001/XMLSchema-instance"
       xmlns:lang="http://www.springframework.org/schema/lang"
       xsi:schemaLocation="http://www.springframework.org/schema/beans
       http://www.springframework.org/schema/beans/spring-beans.xsd
       http://www.springframework.org/schema/lang
       http://www.springframework.org/schema/lang/spring-lang.xsd">

  <lang:groovy name="inline.message">
    <lang:inline-script>
      import md.MessageService

      class inlinegmessage implements MessageService {
        String message
      }
    </lang:inline-script>
    <lang:property name="message" ref="message"/>
  </lang:groovy>
```

```xml
<bean name="message" class="java.lang.String">
  <constructor-arg value="aloha" />
</bean>
</beans>
```

What do we *gain* from this? – primarily flexibility and ease of development. We've been splattering a lot of files everywhere for our configurations and implementation – a common facet of Java development – and here we have a trivial way to shorten the distance between referencing the bean and its actual implementation.

Is this *valuable*? Well, as with so many other things, it depends. It's likely that this is actually a good way to *start* developing such services, as opposed to a final delivery; you can work with a configuration with an inline implementation until it works well enough and then convert it to an external file (as with our other implementations) for refinement, possibly even reloading them as you edit them on disk through the refresh-check-delay attribute in <lang:groovy />.

Of course, we can't just show you the *configuration* without showing you a test. As with Listing 12-9, the test contributes only the configuration filename to the process.

Listing 12-11. chapter12/src/test/java/md/TestInlineMessage.java

```java
package md;

import org.springframework.test.context.ContextConfiguration;
import org.testng.annotations.Test;

@ContextConfiguration(value = "classpath:/inline-context.xml")
@Test
public class TestInlineMessage extends BaseMessageTest {
}
```

Summary

In this chapter, we saw how to use dynamic languages and how they can help you do quick and easy tasks; our task was quite trivial, but you could write anything you needed to, like validating a URL, doing intent analysis through machine learning, anything you're able to express, honestly, leveraging the features of the dynamic language implementation. We demonstrated Groovy here, but *any* dynamic language that meets the JSR-223 specification can be used. We loaded scripts from the classpath and implemented them inline in our configuration, demonstrating a very powerful and easy way to develop behavior on the fly.

CHAPTER 13

Where Do You Go From Here?

What you've read so far has been fairly encompassing for Java application development. We've seen how to build a project, how to configure dependency injection, and how to access data; we've seen how to *present* data over the Web with an actual (but sparse) interface using HTML and template rendering, as well as a REST API; we've seen how to connect to message brokers, how to send (and receive) mail, and how to configure Spring beans using dynamic language scripts on the fly.

What's left?

It turns out that the answer is: nearly everything.

Spring and the Impact on Development

Spring's been around for a long time, coming up on nearly 20 years at the very least, from its earliest development. It's used quite literally by millions of Java developers and has heavily influenced the entire Java ecosystem, from specifications to library implementations and further to application design, by emphasizing and enabling SOLID principles, as described by Robert Martin et al.,[1] which are as follows:

- S – the single-responsibility principle

- O – the open-closed principle

- L – the Liskov substitution principle

- I – the interface segregation principle

---

[1] Martin, Robert C., Michael C. Feathers, Timothy R. Ottinger, and Jeffrey J. Langr. Clean Code A Handbook of Agile Software Craftsmanship. Boston, MA: Pearson Education, Inc, 2016.

© Felipe Gutierrez, Joseph B. Ottinger 2022
F. Gutierrez and J. B. Ottinger, *Introducing Spring Framework 6*, https://doi.org/10.1007/978-1-4842-8637-1_13

- D – the dependency inversion principle

The single-responsibility principle suggests that a class should do one thing and one thing only; if you look back at our data access objects and our web controllers, you'll see that we tended to have tight focus on doing **one** thing: accessing data, or handling input from the Web (and responding to it), or even delegating to our data access classes such that we can add functionality if it's appropriate.

The single-responsibility principle tends to create a structure that has many relatively small classes, but the advantage here is that if you can identify what the class is supposed to do, you can focus solely on doing it well – creating a testable, simple, *reliable* implementation and making *design* of these classes fairly trivial.

The open-closed principle says that classes should be extensible without having to modify the classes themselves. We've used a lot of inheritance in our examples, particularly in tests, where we create base functionality and mutate it to create the environments we need.

The Liskov substitution principle says that subclasses – or implementations – should be fully substitutable for their parent types. This was demonstrated in this book most clearly in the data access and search engine examples, where we had a base type of `Repository` (from Spring) or `SearchEngine` (our custom interface) and we swapped implementations like mad in our tests. Every one of them was presumed to be equivalent in intent, within limits.[2]

The interface segregation principle says that a class should never be forced to implement an interface it doesn't use, nor should dependencies be forced to depend on methods they do not use. We've not demonstrated a violation of the interface segregation principle, but an example would be for the search engine interface in the early to have a mechanism by which it could *write* documents, going unused until we reached a point in the book where we're accepting new data. The search engine had no such method, because *every* implementation would have been forced to include it. We could have designed a `WritingSearchEngine` that extended `SearchEngine` at some point (perhaps Chapter 9, where we finally updated a database from external data); only the implementations of `WritingSearchEngine` would have been required to fulfill the ability to write document references.

---

[2] Sometimes you might ignore Liskov for the purpose of testing, or for *very* special cases.

This creates a lean implementation of classes; again, simplicity is encouraged. It makes everything far easier to design and debug, which makes everyone more effective as programmers.

The dependency inversion principle suggests that our design should depend on *abstractions*. We've used a ton of interfaces and (occasionally) base classes; these are the types that are used, except where we're specifically testing concrete behavior. The dependencies are on the interfaces, not the concrete implementations, which means we're programming to what the interfaces *intend* – to contract rather than to an actual class.

Programming to contract means that we program based on what we're intending to do, rather than how we do it. It's not important to know that searching for a document queries a database – we only want to search for a document. That's the difference between interface and implementation, and Spring does a *fantastic* job of encouraging us to use this principle.

The Wider World of Spring

The funny thing is: this book is an introduction to Spring, but it barely scratches the surface of the wider ecosystem. We've danced from subject to subject like pinballs, generally establishing more complex topics as we've gone along and integrating concepts we've learned from prior chapters, but even so we've done relatively little.

Spring has modules for nearly *everything*. Looking at the Spring Initializr project (`https://start.spring.io`), you can find libraries to help you use GRAPHQL, or HATEOAS, or reactive programming, multiple template engines (including Thymeleaf, which we demonstrated in our example code), a security layer with OAUTH2 or other security implementations, data access to relational systems (through JDBC or JPA, both of which were demonstrated) or NoSQL datastores like MongoDB, access to multiple messaging systems like Artemis or RabbitMQ, Kafka or Apache Camel, batch processing, and much, much more.

And that's *just* the official Spring projects; the open source world adds even more.

Even beyond that, if the feature is able to be built in Java (or accessed from it), Spring's design principles make it easy for you to implement your own services, as with our email services in Chapter 11.[3] Doing things the "Spring way" tends to create easily maintained code with tight focus on design to contract, so even if a Spring project doesn't exist to fulfill what you need, Spring helps you determine what it is you *actually* need and focus on programming *that*, so you end up with composable modules that create a lot of power in your final design.

Where *should* you look further? Well, as usual, it depends.

If you're manipulating data, Spring Data has a number of applicable projects, but your interest will mostly be based on what database you need to work with.

For the Web, you'll want to look at Spring Security, as well as the various rendering engines; you might also want to look at Reactive, although Reactive is going to apply most heavily in very high performance scenarios.

For data processing, you'll look at the other messaging layers like Kafka or RabbitMQ (if you're not using JMS already); the concepts travel across the libraries just like Spring Data concepts apply to each repository type.

The possibilities are endless, and it's fascinating and empowering to explore and grow.

---

[3] It's worth noting, in the pursuit of radical honesty, that the `EmailService` doesn't *quite* follow SOLID principles in the interest of using fewer pages in print.

Index

A, B

Abstractions, 207
Annotation configuration
    component scanning, 46–49
    expensive operation, 47
    helloWorldMessageService(), 46
    Java configuration, 45
    MyDocsConfigurationTest.java, 45, 46
    MyDocsScanConfig class, 49
    MyDocsScanTest, 48
    ScannedSearchEngine, 48
    ScannedSearchEngine.java, 47
Asynchronous processes, 135, 136,
      145, 147
    Async annotation, 181
    ExecutorService thread, 181
    invocation, 180
    multithread invocation, 180
    scheduling events, 182–189

C

Classes/dependencies
    My Documents application, 40
      build.gradle file, 25
      Document.java, 26, 27
      documents, 23
      DocumentType, 25, 26
      getName() method, 28
      requirements, 23, 24
      SearchEngine, 24, 28
      types, 23

spring testing
    AbstractTestNGSpring
      ContextTests, 34
    ContextConfiguration, 34
    dependency injection/modular, 32
    MyDocumentsSpringTest.java, 33
    MyDocumentsTest, 35
    programmatic configuration, 34
    TestConfiguration.java, 35
testing implementation
    API design, 29
    computational/human domain, 28
    MyDocumentsTest.java, 29, 30
    StaticSearchEngine.java, 30, 31

D

Data access objects (DAOs), 89
    object-relational mapping, 107
    project creation
      application.properties, 113
      build.gradle file, 107, 108
      Document.java, 108, 109
      DocumentType.java, 110
      import.sql, 112
      RepositorySearchEngine.java, 111
      SearchEngine structure, 110
    spring data repositories
      DocumentRepository, 115
      findByType method, 115
      MyDocsConfiguration class, 115, 116
      MyDocsTest class, 116, 117

Data access objects (DAOs) (*cont.*)
    parameters, 113
      standardizable operations, 113, 114
Dependency inversion principle, 207
Dynamic languages
  Groovy (*see* Groovy)

E, F

Extensible Markup Language (XML), 94
  attributes, 51, 52
  component scanning, 58
  configuration, 49
  ContextConfiguration annotation, 50
  documents.xml, 50, 51
  dynamic languages, 194
  expanding configuration
    constant data, 53
    doccons.xml, 54
    docdata.xml, 56, 57
    MyDocsXMLConstructor
      Test, 53, 54
    MyDocsXMLDataTest, 55
    namespace, 55
  hierarchical node structure, 51
  MyDocsAllXMLsTest, 59–61
  MyDocsConfig class, 51
  MyDocsXMLTest, 50
  resource files, 75
  scopes, 65
  Thymeleaf, 124
External systems
  application.properties file, 140
  architectural approach, 136
  build.gradle file, 137, 138
  code information, 145
  CommandLineRunner, 143

Document class, 138, 139
DocumentRepository class, 140
HornetQ message, 136
JdbcTemplate class, 136
JmsPublisher class, 142
JmsReceiver file, 141
JmsTemplate, 137
JmsTemplate.send() method, 143
MessageConverter, 142
MyDocsApp class, 144, 145
receiveMessage method, 141
search engine app, 135
spring-messaging and spring-jms
    modules, 136

G, H

Groovy, 193
  build.gradle files, 194, 195
  classpath/filesystem, 195
  components, 194
  constructor arguments, 194
  dynamic languages, 195
  dynamic MessageService interface
    BaseMessageTest class, 198
    getExpectedMessage(), 199
    gmessage, 196
    simple-context.xml, 197
    package declaration, 197
    TestSimpleMessage class, 199
  filesystem, 196
  inline dynamic content
    inline-context, 202
    primarily flexibility, 203
    service implementation, 202
    TestInlineMessage, 203
  MessageService interface, 194, 195

spring MessageService
    boilerplate methods, 200
    cgmessage, 200
    property-context, 200
    TestPropertyMessage, 201

I

Interface segregation principle, 206
Internationalization, 81–85, 125, 128

J, K

Java application development, 205
Java Database Connectivity (JDBC), 174
    build.gradle file, 94, 95
    configuration file, 95
    data access objects (DAOs), 107
    driver/connection, 94
    explicit.xml, 95, 96
    external systems, 136
    import.sql, 98
    jdbc.properties, 97
    JDBCTemplate, 99
    schema.sql, 97
    tutorial/contexts, 94
Java Development Kit (JDK), 4
JavaMail, 29, 165, 169, 170, 174, 175
Java Message Service (JMS), 136–138, 140,
    143, 145, 180
Java programming, 197
JavaScript, 148
Java Virtual Machine (JVM), 165
JDBCTemplate, 95, 99, 103, 104, 119

L

Liskov substitution principle, 205, 206

M, N

My Documents application
    classes/dependencies, 23–28, 40
    Document.java, 38, 39
    DocumentType.java, 38
    getEngine() method, 44
    MyDocsBaseTest.java, 40, 41
    MyDocsJavaTest.java, 44
    populateData() method, 43
    SearchEngine.java, 40
    SearchService implementation, 37
    StaticSearchEngine.java, 42, 43
    TestNG, 40

O

Object-relational mapper, 107
Open-closed principle, 206

P, Q

Persistence connections
    concepts, 89
    data model, 90–93
    Document/DocumentType, 90–93
    equals() and hashCode()
        methods, 90
    error handling, 90
    idiomatic Java approach, 89
    JDBC driver, 94–99
    MyDocsTest.java, 104–106
    relational databases, 90, 93
    SearchEngine interface, 100–104
    search engine
        implementation, 104–106
Programmatic configuration, *see*
        Annotation configuration

R

REpresentational State Transfer (REST)
   application.properties, 158
   build.gradle file, 149
   class definition, 161
   @Controller annotation, 148
   ControllerTest, 158–161
   definition, 147
   DELETE, 148
   DocumentController, 153–155
   document file, 147, 149–151
   DocumentRepository file, 151, 155
   findAll() method, 151, 152
   getForEntity() method, 162
   GET method, 156
   HTTP methods, 156
   import.sql, 157, 158
   loadDocument() method, 155
   MyDocsApp, 152
   post()/put() methods, 156
   PUT/POST requests, 147
   ResponseStatus annotation, 155
   RestController annotation, 148
   server error, 156
   testDeleteDocument() method, 163
   testGetBadDocument() method, 162
   testGetDocument() method, 162
   testPostDocument() method, 163
   testPutDocument()/
      testPutDocumentWithBadId()
      methods, 163
   TestRestTemplate class, 161
   URL path, 156
   utility methods, 162
Resource files
   external files, 75
   injecting configuration
      build.gradle file, 75
      getContent() method, 78
      hello.txt file, 76
      loading process, 78
      property files, 78–85
      ResourceInjectionTest file, 76, 77
   internationalization, 81–85
   property files
      classpath, 79
      inject values, 78
      menu.properties, 80
      PropertySource annotation, 81
      PropertySource/Value
        annotation, 79
      PropertyTest.java, 80, 81
      SpEL method, 79, 80
REST APIs, 147–164

S

Scheduling events
   CrontabMonitorService, 187, 188
   elapsed-rate system, 182
   equivalent expressions, 187
   events, 182
   expressions, 186
   fields, 186
   fixed-rate system, 182
   FixedRateMonitorService, 183, 184
   fixedRateTest(), 185
   isWorking() method, 184
   start() method, 182, 184
   SystemMonitor service, 182
   TestCrontabService, 189
   TestFixedRateService, 185
   time system, 182
   updateWorkingState()
      method, 184

Scopes
    annotations, 73–74
    assertEquals, 69
    build.gradle file, 65
    class configuration, 72
    classpath pattern, 69
    components, 69
    constructor-arg, 70–72
    consumer class, 66, 67
    execute() methods, 70
    getValue() method, 69
    log execution, 72, 73
    meaning, 63
    Producer.java, 66
    prototype, 70
    ScopesTest class, 67–69
    settings.gradle file, 65
    singleton and prototype, 64
    web applications, 63–65
Service/SearchEngine interfaces
    DocumentDAO.java, 100
    DocumentJDBCDAO, 102–104
    DocumentMapper, 103
    implementation, 100
    SearchEngine.java, 100
    SearchEngineService, 101
Sending/receiving email, 165
    JavaMail, 165
    JavaMailSender, 165
    MailTrap, 166–167
    project descriptor
        access method, 175
        application.properties, 169
        build.gradle file, 168
        cascading methods, 175
        checkReceiveEmailFromInbox()
          method, 179
        deleteMessage() method, 176

        EmailService, 170–174, 176, 180
        EmailService.processMessages()
          method, 179
        environment variables, 168
        getMessages() method, 175, 176
        JavaMail, 174, 175
        JavaMailSender, 169, 174
        matching message, 180
        POP3, 170
        processMessages() method, 175
        send() method, 174
        TestConfiguration, 177
        TestEmailService, 177–179
    SMTP configuration settings, 167
Single-responsibility principle, 206
Spring application, 37
    annotation configuration, 45–60
    Boot
        build.gradle file, 14
        features, 14
        HelloWorldController, 16–18
        HelloWorldController.java, 15, 16
        HTTP requests, 17
        settings.gradle file, 15
    configuration approach, 60
    data access objects (DAOs), 107–117
    dependency inversion principle, 207
    dynamic languages, 193–203
    dynamic language scripts, 205
    email (*see* Sending/receiving email)
    external systems, 135–146
    Gradle Website, 5
    Hello World
        Application.java, 12
        build.gradle file, 10
        component type, 13
        execution process, 13
        getMessage() method, 11

Spring application (*cont.*)
    HelloService.java, 11, 12
    message service, 11
    modular code, 14
    source code, 10
  history, 3
  interface segregation principle, 206
  Kotlin information
    build.gradle file, 19
    HelloWorldController.kt, 20
    settings.gradle, 19
  Liskov substitution principle, 206
  modules, 207, 208
  open-closed principle, 206
  persistence concepts, 89–106
  portfolio website, 3
  pre-requirements, 4–5
  REST (*see* REpresentational State
    Transfer (REST))
  scope (*see* Scopes)
  single-responsibility
    principle, 206
  SOLID principles, 205
  source code organization, 5
    build.gradle file, 6
    directory tree, 9
    Gradle project, 6
    setting.gradle file, 7–9
    top-level project, 6
  testing, 32–35
  web application, 119–120
  wider ecosystem, 207–208
Spring Expression Language (SpEL), 79
Synchronous processes, 135

T, U, V

Thymeleaf, 119, 148
  application source code, 128
  expression language, 126
  getName() method, 127
  hello.text property, 126
  internationalization, 128
  messages, 125, 127
  namespaces, 124
  rendered page, 128–131
  search/all, 125
  search page, 130
  switch languages, 131
  templates, 125

W

Web application
  build script, 119, 120
  Controller, 121
  ControllerTest, 123, 124
  data storage, 119
  directory structure, 120, 121
  listAll()/searchAll() methods, 123, 124
  model-view-controller
    paradigm, 122
  SearchController, 122
  spring data, 119
  Thymeleaf (*see* Thymeleaf)

X, Y, Z

XML, *see* Extensible Markup
  Language (XML)

Printed in the United States
by Baker & Taylor Publisher Services